The American Revolution

NBC REGIONAL MEDIA CENTER
COLUMBUS, N.J. 08022

AMERICAN HISTORY

The American Revolution

John Davenport

LUCENT BOOKS

An imprint of Thomson Gale, a part of The Thomson Corporation

Detroit • New York • San Francisco • New Haven, Conn. • Waterville, Maine • London

For more information, contact
Lucent Books
27500 Drake Rd.
Farmington Hills, MI 48331-3535
Or you can visit our Internet site at http://www.gale.com

LIBRARY OF CONGRESS CATALOGING-IN-PUBLICATION DATA

Davenport, John, 1960–
 The American Revolution / by John Davenport.
  p. cm. — (American history)
 Includes bibliographical references and index.
 ISBN-13: 978-1-59018-939-9 (hard cover : alk. paper)
 1. United States—History—Revolution, 1775–1783—Juvenile literature. 2. United States—History—Revolution, 1775–1783—Causes—Juvenile literature. I. Title.
 E208.D155 2007
 973.3'11—dc22
                                                                                    2006007348

ISBN-10: 1-59018-939-6

Printed in the United States of America

Foreword

The United States has existed as a nation for just over 200 years. By comparison, Rome existed as a nation-state for more than 1000 years. Out of a few struggling British colonies, the United States developed relatively quickly into a world power whose policy decisions and culture have great influence on the world stage. What events and aspirations drove this young American nation to such great heights in such a short period of time? The answer lies in a close study of its varied and unique history. As James Baldwin once remarked, "American history is longer, larger, more various, more beautiful, and more terrible than anything anyone has ever said about it."

The basic facts of United States history—names, dates, places, battles, treaties, speeches, and acts of Congress—fill countless textbooks. These facts, though essential to a thorough understanding of world events, are rarely compelling for students. More compelling are the stories in history, the experience of history.

Titles in this series explore the history of the country and the experiences of Americans. What influences led the colonists to risk everything and break from Britain? Who was the driving force behind the Constitution? Which factors led thousands of people to leave their homelands and settle in the United States? Questions like these do not have simple answers; by discussing them, however, we can view the past as a more real, interesting, and accessible place.

Students will find excellent tools for research and investigation in every title. Lucent Books' American History series provides not only facts, but also the analysis and context necessary for insightful critical thinking about history and about current events. Fully cited quotations from historical figures, eyewitnesses, letters, speeches, and writings bring vibrancy and authority to the text. Annotated bibliographies allow students to evaluate and locate sources for further investigation. Sidebars highlight important and interesting figures, events, or related primary source excerpts. Timelines, maps, and full color images add another dimension of accessibility to the stories being told.

It has been said the past has a history of repeating itself, for good and ill. In these pages, students will learn a bit about both and, perhaps, better understand their own place in this world.

Important Dates at the Time

1768
James Cook leaves England on a three-year quest to sail around the world, during which he discovers Australia.

1775
James Watt invents the steam engine.

1760
George III becomes king of Great Britain.

1766
Famine breaks out in the Bengal region of India.

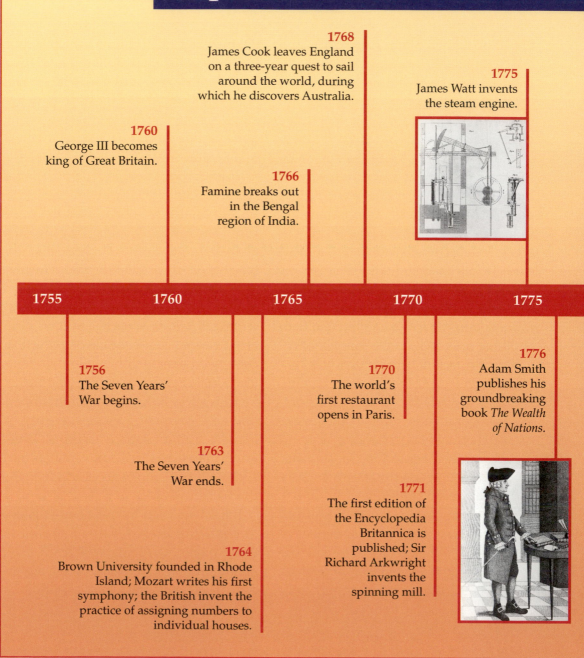

1755	1760	1765	1770	1775

1756
The Seven Years' War begins.

1770
The world's first restaurant opens in Paris.

1776
Adam Smith publishes his groundbreaking book *The Wealth of Nations.*

1763
The Seven Years' War ends.

1771
The first edition of the Encyclopedia Britannica is published; Sir Richard Arkwright invents the spinning mill.

1764
Brown University founded in Rhode Island; Mozart writes his first symphony; the British invent the practice of assigning numbers to individual houses.

of the American Revolution

1777
The first American flag is officially designated by Congress.

1779
The British go to war against the independent Marathas in India; the first early bicycles appear on the streets of Paris.

1777	1778	1779	1780	1781	1782	1783	1784

1780
The fountain pen is invented.

1783
The Montgolfier brothers take flight in the first successful hot-air balloon.

1778
The famous Enlightenment philosophers Jean-Jacques Rousseau and François-Marie Voltaire both die; Captain Cook discovers Hawaii.

A Troubled Family

The imperial relationship between Great Britain and its American colonies was perhaps the most tense and conflict-ridden in history. Constant trouble marred its development, and arguments between the parent country and colonies over one matter or another were frequent. From the establishment of Jamestown in 1607 right up to the Declaration of Independence in 1776, the imperial partners quarreled incessantly. Americans and Britons alike felt misunderstood and ill used. Americans believed that 3,000 miles (4,828km) of ocean and 150 years of history put too much distance between them and their English counterparts. People back in Britain, Americans generally agreed, no longer shared their interests or problems. Britons, both inside and outside of the government ministries, looked at the colonists and saw spoiled and ungrateful children who lacked a decent respect for parliament and the king.

Sentiments such as those above were more common with each passing year. They also became tinged with suspicion and mistrust. Disagreement and animosity grew. Eventually, antagonism tore the empire apart, sending Great Britain and its former colonies in separate directions. Yet from its imperial ruins emerged a new nation "among the powers of the earth," as the Declaration of Independence proclaimed; an independent United States of America.

Trade

The first tear in the fabric of empire appeared in the area of trade. Economics has always taken center stage in transatlantic relations between America and Britain. The earliest English settlements, in fact, had been set up explicitly to promote trade. As one sixteenth-century promoter of colonization said to Queen Elizabeth I, in America "her Majesty and her subjects may both enjoy the treasures of mines of silver and gold and the whole trade . . . filling Her Majesty's coffers to the full."[1] England needed the raw materials and potential markets that only colonies could provide. The resulting settlements, for their part, had to have a buyer for the timber, molasses, grain, hides, and other products of the land offered in abundance by America. Commercial connections between the colonies and the homeland, augmented later by intercolonial trade, met the needs of both partners. It also turned a handsome profit for each.

This cooperative arrangement flourished for a time, but beginning in the 1730s it showed signs of breaking down. From the middle of the seventeenth century on, the home government had been putting restrictions on imperial trade. It realized that, as the modern economic historians John J. McCusker and Russell R. Menard explain, England's "trade, both imports and exports, depended upon the colonists as producers and consumers."[2] Parliament thus passed a series of Navigation Acts in 1651, 1660, 1663, and 1673. These were commercial laws designed to protect the imperial economy by forcing the colonies to trade only with Britain or other British colonies. In almost every case, Americans responded to the laws by ignoring them.

American merchants routinely evaded trade restrictions by smuggling goods in and out of colonial ports. Few American traders felt compelled to obey laws written in faraway London, especially if they lost money by doing so. Worse yet, some of the smuggled cargo came from French ports in the West Indies. Considering how often Britain and France were at war, this constituted treason in some Britons' minds. Royal officials often charged Americans with being disloyal as well as dishonest. By the 1750s, if not earlier, trade had become a sore spot in imperial relations. More than an ocean, it seemed, separated the British and the Americans when it came to commerce.

Shown here is a facsimile of the Declaration of Independence.

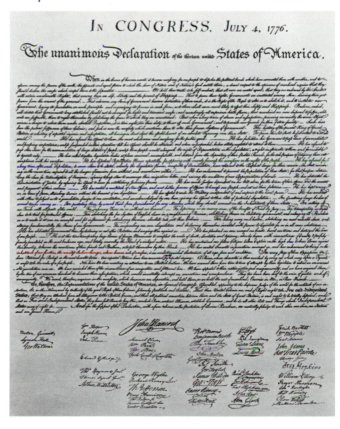

Politics

Britain and the colonies disagreed bitterly over trade policies. They clashed no less furiously over the issue of legislative sovereignty. Political leaders sitting in London and their counterparts in the colonial capitals argued about exactly who could legitimately write laws for America. The British contended that only parliament had the power to pass laws applying to British subjects, no matter where they lived. Americans, on the other hand, claimed that local legislatures and no other body had the authority to craft and pass legislation for the colonies.

These conflicting assertions led ultimately to what the historian Edmund Morgan calls, "a confrontation between the sovereignty of the peoples' representatives in England and the peoples' representatives in the colonies."[3] No state could have two legislative centers of power. Sooner or later the question of where sovereignty was located would have to be answered. Either parliament or the colonial legislatures would have to be given the final say in very impor-

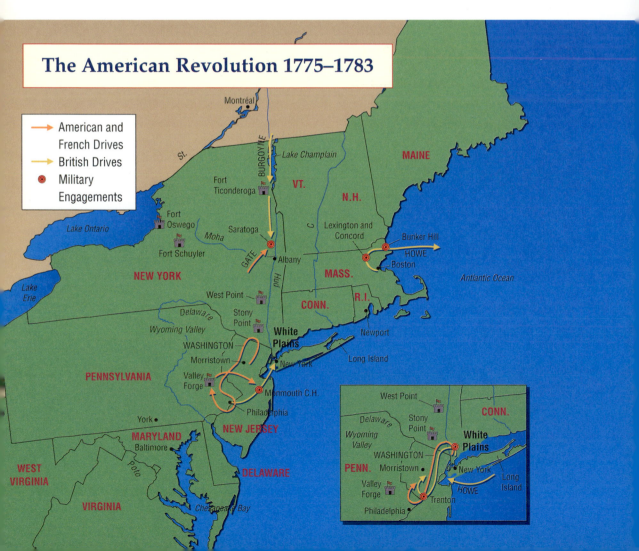

The American Revolution 1775–1783

American and French Drives
British Drives
Military Engagements

Montréal
St.
Lake Champlain
BURGOYNE
Fort Ticonderoga
VT.
MAINE
N.H.
Fort Oswego
Saratoga
Moha
Lexington and Concord
Bunker Hill
Lake Ontario
Fort Schuyler
GATE
Albany
HOWE
Boston
MASS.
Antlantic Ocean
Lake Erie
NEW YORK
West Point
Hud
CONN.
R.I.
Delaware
Stony Point
Newport
Wyoming Valley
WASHINGTON
White Plains
Long Island
Morristown
New York
PENNSYLVANIA
Valley Forge
Monmouth C.H.
Philadelphia
York
NEW JERSEY
MARYLAND
Baltimore
DELAWARE
WEST VIRGINIA
Poto
VIRGINIA
Chesapeake Bay

West Point
Delaware
Stony Point
CONN.
Wyoming Valley
White Plains
WASHINGTON
PENN.
Morristown
New York
Valley Forge
HOWE
Long Island
Trenton
Philadelphia

tant matters, perhaps the most important being taxation.

War

The contest over legislative authority was a war of words, but real wars were a routine occurrence in early America. Bloodshed was something with which colonial Americans were all too familiar. A colonist born in 1690 who was lucky enough to live to the age of eighty would have witnessed four major imperial wars and countless smaller ones. In most of these conflicts, Britons and Americans had marched into battle side by side. Such shared danger and hardship should have built camaraderie and reinforced a feeling of mutual "Englishness." Instead, colonial warfare bred distrust and disdain, not for the French, their common enemy, but for each other.

British officers and men who fought in North America considered the militias and provincial armies beside them to be inferior in quality and fighting spirit. The Americans, the British said derisively, lacked soldierly ability and drive. The colonials were, in short, cast in the role of ill-disciplined amateurs. In British eyes, the Americans were "vagabonds . . . the lowest dregs . . . on which no dependence could be had . . . the scum of the worst people."[4]

The colonial militiamen saw things differently. British officers, they sniffed, were little more than elite snobs who neither earned nor merited command. When it came to British enlisted men, Americans accused them of being illiterate drones "unacquainted with the American way of war." Ineffective against Indians and given to criminality, so it was rumored, the British soldier was prone to "dastardly behavior [and] deadly panic." Capping off the criticism, American soldiers claimed that they fought for family and community, "not like the regulars, for pay."[5] Both sides underestimated their future opponents.

A Darkening Horizon

War, politics, trade, and a host of other indicators pointed toward a violent rupture in imperial relations. The differences and disagreements between Great Britain and its American colonies grew to proportions that made some sort of conflict inevitable. Yet common threats and timely compromises always seemed to hold the empire together. Crises were viewed as family squabbles within an imperial household that had dangerous foes just outside the door. Only with the defeat of France in 1763 was the most threatening of those foes removed. After nine years of fighting in North America, Great Britain was supreme on the continent. Absent any external challenge, Americans and Britons were free to settle internal matters once and for all. Neither really thought that they would do this by turning their muskets away from the foreign enemy and toward each other.

Chapter One

Sugar and Stamps, 1763–1766

The Seven Years' War (1756–1763) represented the final act in a global drama. It was the climax of a decades-long struggle between Great Britain and France for European influence and dominion over North America. Breaking out in America in 1754 as the French and Indian War and spreading to Europe two years later, the war resulted in a stunning and complete British victory. That victory, oddly enough, marked the beginning of the end for the united British empire. In that sense, the British lost far more than they gained.

Keeping the Peace: The Proclamation Line of 1763

At the time, however, it appeared that Britain had won quite a bit. The Treaty of Paris that brought the conflict to a close transferred immense tracts of land to the British. By the treaty's terms, France ceded Canada, Florida, and all of the territory between the Appalachian Mountains and the Mississippi River to Great Britain. In order to cut the cost of defending this newly won domain, the British parliament drew up the Proclamation of 1763.

Enacted in October of that year, the Proclamation declared the British intention to bring peace to "all our loving subjects . . . in America."[6] The peace would be ensured by limiting contact between Indians and colonists. In fact, a line was drawn on the map of North America that ran along the spine of the Appalachian Mountains. The colonists would stay on one side, the Indians on the other. Any settlers already in Indian territory would have "to remove themselves from such settlements" immediately.[7] In return for moving out, Americans were promised that Indians would no longer be sold guns and that thousands of British troops would be assigned to protect frontier towns and villages.

Indian Trouble

The British trusted that the line they drew on a map in London would prevent future conflicts in America. It might have done just that if news of the proclamation had reached the colonies earlier. By the time it did, blood was already flowing once more.

Angered by British refusal to engage in trade and act as intertribal mediators, as the French had done, and insulted by the gun ban, Indians along the frontier rose up. Led by an Ottawa warrior named Pontiac, the Indians launched a ferocious assault on American settlements and

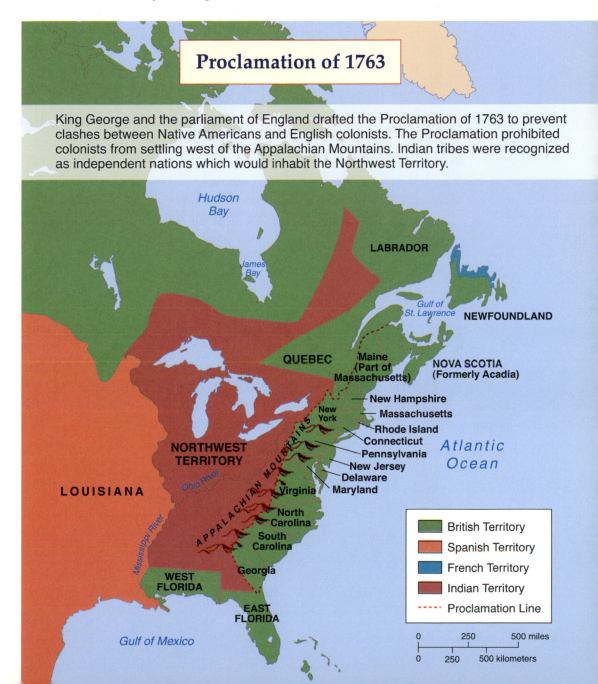

Proclamation of 1763

King George and the parliament of England drafted the Proclamation of 1763 to prevent clashes between Native Americans and English colonists. The Proclamation prohibited colonists from settling west of the Appalachian Mountains. Indian tribes were recognized as independent nations which would inhabit the Northwest Territory.

Hudson Bay

James Bay

LABRADOR

Gulf of St. Lawrence

NEWFOUNDLAND

QUEBEC

Maine (Part of Massachusetts)

NOVA SCOTIA (Formerly Acadia)

New Hampshire
Massachusetts
New York
Rhode Island
Connecticut
Pennsylvania
New Jersey
Delaware
Maryland

NORTHWEST TERRITORY

Ohio River

APPALACHIAN MOUNTAINS

Virginia

Atlantic Ocean

LOUISIANA

Mississippi River

North Carolina

South Carolina

Georgia

WEST FLORIDA

EAST FLORIDA

Gulf of Mexico

	British Territory
	Spanish Territory
	French Territory
	Indian Territory
-----	Proclamation Line

0   250   500 miles
0   250   500 kilometers

British forts in May 1763. The colonial response was swift and bloody. Animated by racial bigotry and frustration at the parent country's seeming indifference to their plight, frontiersmen attacked Indian villages and hounded Indian war parties.

Ottawa warrior Pontiac led the Indians on an attack against the Americans and British.

The Americans, however, saved enough energy to point an accusatory finger at the home government. Settlers claimed that the proclamation line protected murderers and savages. It also crushed the hopes of colonial farmers who desperately needed access to western land. The presence of British regulars along the line also aroused old fears of tyranny. Royal soldiers, it was claimed, could be used to enforce laws that Americans disagreed with. The redcoats might even be part of a scheme to deny the colonists their rights as British subjects. In any case, colonial patience was wearing thin. Parliament, Americans complained, seemed to be "in favour of Indians only, against His Majesty's faithful & loyal subjects" east of the disputed line.[8] Colonial suspicions grew.

Money from Sugar

Parliament, at the height of the war with Pontiac, did little to ease American fears. In fact, it passed a piece of trade legislation that only made matters worse. The Indian campaign was in full swing and American tempers were rising. It was not a good time to begin addressing the debt left over from the war with France. Nine years of fighting had been expensive; the national debt of Great Britain in 1763 stood at approximately $12 billion in modern money and was rising. Much of this amount reflected expenditures on

Samuel Adams

Samuel Adams's career took him from work as a local brewer to the role of fiery revolutionary and finally to public office in the state of Massachusetts. Born in Boston in 1722, Adams's first public job was as a tax collector. He was renowned for such lax enforcement that he ended up being fired. Moving from government employee to government official, Adams was elected to the Massachusetts House of Representatives in 1765. At the same time, he helped found the Loyal Nine, the organization that evolved into the Sons of Liberty. His exploits over the next five years put Adams in the forefront of the radical movement against parliamentary rule. Between 1770 and 1773 Adams kept the resistance alive in Massachusetts, battling all the while with Governor Thomas Hutchinson for influence among a people inching toward open rebellion. Adams became a prominent figure outside of New England in 1774, when he began a six-year term in the Continental Congress. As the fighting moved south in 1780, Adams returned to Massachusetts to help write the new state's first constitution. His service continued after the war, with Adams serving first as lieutenant governor (1789–1793) and then as governor (1793–1797). After a long and often tumultuous career, Samuel Adams died in 1803.

either the war or colonial defense. The overall debt was slowing the British economy on its own, but new spending for the military in America was compounding the problem on a monthly basis. Parliament, in short, needed to raise money in a hurry.

Taxation was the obvious solution, but imposing new taxes on an already overburdened British middle class would be very unpopular. Taxpayers at home might become more hostile than the enemies abroad. An alternative, however, presented itself. Parliament could move to enforce existing trade restrictions and curtail smuggling between North America and the West Indies. Smuggling was big business in coastal cities and towns, and no product was traded illegally as often as molasses, despite the passage of an antismuggling law in 1733. The Molasses Act of that year placed a six-cent duty on each gallon of molasses imported into America and limited purchases to those from British suppliers.

The problem only got worse. Molasses, derived from boiled sugar, was the main ingredient in rum. This alcoholic beverage was in high demand in the mid-eighteenth century. It was a valuable commodity and represented a key component in the slave trade that was booming at the time. With over 127 distilleries dotting New England, molasses was often in short supply and thus commanded premium prices. Illegally importing molasses, therefore, became the preferred way to lower production costs and maximize profits. No sooner had the act been passed, however, than colonial traders began smuggling molasses with abandon.

By 1763 rampant smuggling, aided by lax enforcement, was costing the royal treasury huge sums of money each year. Less than 5 percent of the income that should have resulted from the molasses duty actually made it into King George III's coffers. The rest ended up in colonial pockets. This was money that parliament was determined to get back.

After several government investigations confirmed that the molasses duty was essentially uncollected, parliament passed the Sugar Act of 1764. Followed closely by the Currency Act, a law that prohibited the colonies from printing their own money, the Sugar Act took a carrot-and-stick approach to raising revenue. The carrot was a substantial lowering of the molasses duty from six cents to three. It would later be reduced to a mere penny per gallon (3.8L). The stick was that the Sugar Act would be scrupulously enforced. The illegal trade would be choked off by the royal navy, which was granted the authority to seize smugglers' ships and impound them. The owners of these vessels were required to appear not in local court but in a special naval court in Halifax, Nova Scotia, to petition for the return of their property. This provision was designed to prevent bribery and cor-ruption. Taken together, it became clear that parliament intended to collect the money that it felt was rightfully due and use it to offset the cost of defending the colonies.

A Bitter Reaction

Parliament saw nothing in the Sugar Act for Americans to complain about. The evasion of the molasses duty was threatening the kingdom's economic health. Anyway, it was argued, honest, law-abiding citizens had no need to worry; only smugglers and deceitful distillers would be impacted. The colonial elite, particularly New Englanders who benefited from the illegal trade, saw matters differently. They protested that parliament was exceeding its authority by using the military to enforce trade laws. Colonial leaders, furthermore, accused the home government of concocting a scheme to strangle American trade and hobble a vibrant and growing colonial economy. Samuel Adams, a prominent Boston brewer soon to become America's premier radical, warned ominously that the Sugar Act was only the first step on the road to tyranny. "For if our trade may be taxed," he reasoned, "why not our lands? Why not the produce of our lands and, in short, everything we possess or make use of?"[9]

Clearly exaggerating, Adams hoped that his words would inflame average colonists. He wanted to convince them to rise up and defend the interests of those who profited from molasses smuggling. Unfortunately for Adams and others like him, the Sugar Act did not directly affect most Americans. Only a minority of colonists would experience any real hardship with the act's implementation. Try though they did, the future revolutionary leadership could not rouse the colonist on the street to action.

The Furor over Some Stamps

The Sugar Act failed to provoke a mass response that crossed class lines. Those

George III (shown here), was king of England during the American Revolution.

who protested it did so without the support of the crowd. Adams and his compatriots could not forge a link between their interests and those of their working-class neighbors. Luckily for them, parliament was about to pass another law that would create just such a connection.

In late 1764 Sir George Grenville, George III's prime minister, proposed a special tax for America. The tax was intended to defray the cost of defending the colonies from French or Spanish attack. It would simultaneously relieve British taxpayers of that burden. The tax would come in the form of royal stamps that Americans would have to buy in order to do business legally. The stamps had to appear on an array of commonplace public documents including deeds, licenses of various kinds, legal records, clearance papers for ships, even decks of playing cards. If approved by parliament, Grenville's Stamp Act would go into effect in March 1765.

The proposed bill made perfect sense in England. The stamp tax would reduce the national debt and prod the Americans into paying for their own protection. True, the revenue generated by stamp sales would cover only 30 percent of the total amount needed, but a companion bill, the Quartering Act, would require Americans to cover the costs of supporting troops already stationed in the colonies. Together, the Stamp and

Quartering Acts would ensure that the burden of empire would be more equitably distributed between British subjects at home and abroad.

The Americans React

The Stamp Act's reception in America was far worse than expected. A tax levied only on some of the king's loyal subjects seemed grossly unfair. Americans wondered why they should be singled out to pay for imperial maintenance. Unlike the Sugar Act, moreover, the new revenue measure impacted every American in one way or another. No matter what one's social status might be, stamps would have to be purchased.

The Pennsylvania Journal Advertiser *created this fake stamp to express their opposition to the Stamp Act.*

One by one, colonial legislatures issued formal protests against the Stamp Act. By June 1765 most colonies had made their voices heard. Perhaps the loudest was that of Virginia. There the House of Burgesses declared that local assemblies had "the only and sole right to lay taxes" on the colonists they represented. Only "the people themselves or . . . persons chosen by themselves" could determine a proper system of taxation.[10] The cry of "no taxation without representation" had been heard for the first time but not the last.

As the protests spread, legislators began to speak of a united reply to a measure that troubled them all. They urged the meeting of a special colonial congress, a Stamp Act Congress, which would answer parliament in unison. In October 1765 just such a meeting was held in New York City. Twenty-eight delegates attended the congress, representing nine colonies. When they had finished their work, a set of resolutions lay ready for the king and parliament to read. In sum, the congress told the king that the Stamp Act "by imposing taxes on the inhabitants of these colonies . . . [has] a manifest tendency to subvert the rights and liberties of the colonists." The delegates, moreover, stated their belief that "no taxes [should] be imposed on them but with their consent."[11] The point was made; liberty was based upon

Colonists protest against the Stamp Act, August 1765.

the idea of a free people governing—and taxing— themselves.

Riots and Radicals

While some colonists talked, others took more concrete action. Convinced that parliament was plotting to undermine colonial freedom, Americans began to form loose radical organizations. The first and most energetic appeared in Boston. Known as the Loyal Nine, it was a group composed of local merchants and craftsmen

Thomas Hutchinson

Perhaps America's most famous and ill-starred loyalist, Thomas Hutchinson was born in Boston in 1711. His family's Massachusetts roots extended back nearly one hundred years. His ancestors included the religious reformer Anne Hutchinson. After studying law and history, Hutchinson entered public service in 1737. He began as a colonial representative and rose to become lieutenant governor. Throughout the crisis years of the 1760s and 1770s, Hutchinson's loyalties were torn between his home and his king. He paid dearly for this; Hutchinson was mistrusted by both sides. For three arduous and lonely years, from 1771 to 1774, he worked as colonial governor to keep the empire together, at least in Massachusetts. His efforts came to nothing, and Hutchinson reluctantly emigrated to England when the Revolution began. There he wrote a history of Massachusetts and advised successive governments on American affairs. Hutchinson died in January 1781. His obituary in a Boston newspaper summed up Hutchinson's life, saying that he "was born to be the cause and the victim of popular fury, outrage, and conflagration." Like many other loyalists, Thomas Hutchinson suffered for his devotion to both America and Great Britain.

Quoted in Bernard Bailyn, *The Ordeal of Thomas Hutchinson.* Cambridge, MA: Belknap Press of Harvard University Press, 1974, p. 375.

dedicated to keeping the hated stamps off the streets. Led by Samuel Adams, the Loyal Nine directed its most furious attacks against the men who had the job of implementing parliament's measure—Governor Francis Bernard, Lieutenant governor Thomas Hutchinson, and stamp distributor Andrew Oliver. The lieutenant governor, being a native-born American, suffered being labeled a virtual traitor. As historian Bernard Bailyn relates, "no one in America had been as deliberately and savagely assaulted as Hutchinson [even though] he had opposed the Stamp Act."[12]

The angry words directed at Hutchinson, and through him at the Stamp Act itself, soon led to violence. Inflamed by the fierce rhetoric of the Loyal Nine, the people of Boston formed a mob on the morning of August 14, 1765. Moving through the quiet streets to the city wharf, the crowd destroyed the building where it was reported that the stamps would be kept. The people then proceeded to Oliver's house, carrying an effigy of the distributor. When they arrived, they cut off the mannequin's head, burned its body, and shattered the building's windows. These antics were an unmistakable warning to Oliver.

Twelve days later another mob came dangerously close to open rebellion against British authority. Oliver, having wisely resigned his post, was safe for the time being. This time the target of the crowd's fury was Hutchinson. In the nighttime darkness of August 26, Hutchinson's house was demolished just moments after the lieutenant governor and his family had fled for their lives. The mob also destroyed or looted, in today's money, close to $120,000 worth of personal property. The next day Hutchinson went to a local magistrate and reiterated his opposition to the Stamp Act. He then lamented, "how easy it is for some designing, wicked men to spread false reports, raise suspicions and jealousies in the minds of the populace and enrage them against the innocent."[13] Those "wicked men" would soon be called the Sons of Liberty.

The Resistance Spreads

Boston was only the beginning. By the end of August, rioting had broken out in Newport, Rhode Island, forcing the resignation of the stamp distributor there. Beyond New England, radical groups began springing up throughout the colonies. Everywhere stamp officers were bullied into quitting their jobs. The intimidation was so severe that by the November start date no one dared serve as a distributor. In those places where stamps had been off-loaded from ships, they were destroyed by mobs. Most of the stamps destined for America, in fact, never made it off the ships that carried them.

The Stamp Act was effectively dead. When large numbers of colonists began boycotting British goods, trade and the home economy began to suffer. Parliament, its own membership now divided on the issue of American taxation, was unable to control the situation. Bernard summed up matters in America in a letter to the Board of Trade: "The real authority of government is at an end."[14]

Repeal—with One Condition

News of the turmoil in America soon reached London and the waiting ears of

Lieutenant governor Thomas Hutchinson was a loyalist who was torn between America and Great Britain.

a new British prime minister. Displeased with Grenville, George III had replaced him with Charles Watson-Wentworth, Marquis of Rockingham. Rockingham had never been an ardent supporter of the Stamp Act and was well aware of its potential economic and political costs. If he needed any reminding, it was provided by the merchants of London, who in January 1766 formally urged the repeal of the Stamp Act. Turning to a supposed expert on American temperament, Benjamin Franklin, Rockingham and parliament were told that the colonists would never accept any tax that affected their internal business. Trade laws were one thing; a tax on daily life was another.

Rockingham, seeing no other way out, moved to repeal the Stamp Act. He did so, however, with an eye on maintaining parliament's overall authority. The end product was the Declaratory Act, in which repeal was coupled with a clear statement of parliament's sovereignty. The American colonies, the act read, "have been, are, and of right ought to be subordinate unto,

Molasses: Black Gold

Derived from the sugar grown throughout the Caribbean, molasses, a runny black syrup, was far more prized than sugar itself. When processed by boiling (distillation), molasses yielded rum, the slightly sweet and highly alcoholic beverage that was an important colonial product. Rum was exported mainly from New England to other colonies and Great Britain. It was crucial to the so-called "triangular trade" in slaves. Along with iron, cloth, and firearms, rum was exchanged for slaves in Africa who were then sent to the Caribbean to grow sugar that was transported north to make rum. The rum was eventually traded for more slaves, and the vicious cycle began anew. The booming trade in humans meant that molasses production soared. In 1770 the island of Barbados alone produced over 1 million gallons (3.8 million L) of molasses that was distilled into over 2 million gallons (7.6 million L) of rum. The West Indies turned out an astonishing 11 million gallons (42 million L) of molasses, most of which was destined for the rum market. The noted economic historians John J. McCusker and Russell R. Menard have argued that overall economic development in the colonial West Indies "can be largely related to the spread effects not so much of sugar as of molasses and rum." The fact that the American economy came to depend on slave labor lent a bitter history to something so sweet.

John J. McCusker and Russell R. Menard, *The Economy of British America, 1607–1789.* Chapel Hill: University of North Carolina Press, 1985, p. 166.

and dependent upon the imperial crown and Parliament of Great Britain . . . [which could] make laws and statutes . . . to bind the colonies and people of America . . . in all cases whatsoever.[15] On March 4, 1766, after vigorous debate, the House of Commons passed both the repeal and the Declaratory Act. Seven days later, the House of Lords did likewise, and on March 18 George III gave his approval. The acts covering molasses, currency, and the quartering of troops were left in place—the seeds of future trouble.

The British had misjudged their American cousins' reaction to the assertion of parliamentary power. The Sugar and Stamp Acts had produced not only popular resentment and resistance, but also organized radicalism. Born out of the Loyal Nine, the Sons of Liberty grew to become an intercolonial model of coordinated anti-British action. Americans, thanks to the missteps of men in London, now possessed the means to oppose efforts to control them, their society, and their destiny.

Chapter Two

From Townsend to Tea, 1767–1773

The tensions generated by the Stamp Act were still running high when parliament decided to test American resolve and prove its own. In the Declaratory Act, parliament stated clearly its determination to pass laws, especially economic ones, for America. It had also not abandoned the idea of forcing Americans to pay for their own defense. Americans were British subjects, parliament argued, and they should contribute to the maintenance of Britain's empire.

Many Britons, inside and outside of the halls of parliament, felt this way; chancellor of the exchequer Charles Townsend certainly did. Given the task of managing Britain's economy, Townsend felt confident that he could wring from the colonies the revenue that had eluded Grenville. Plagued by epilepsy and near poverty his whole life, Townsend had little sympathy for American complaints about hardship. Each year the cost of pro-

tecting America grew larger. Townsend set himself to the job of making the colonists pay for that service.

In May 1767 Townsend laid before parliament an ambitious plan to raise money for America from Americans. Called the Revenue Act, the bill spelled out a program of duties to make "a more certain and adequate provision for defraying . . . the expenses of defending, protecting, and securing"[16] the colonies. The plan included import duties on a range of products from paper, paint, lead, and glass to tea. These commodities came directly from England and therefore could not be easily smuggled. Still, the Revenue Act reiterated the royal navy's role in antismuggling operations. Enforcement of the act's provisions would be the job of a new American Board of Customs Commissioners. The ABCC would answer directly to authorities in London, allowing it to avoid dealing with corrupt local officials and courts.

Finally, the money derived from the duties would be used in part to pay the salaries of governors and other royal officers in the colonies. A curious attachment to a revenue act, this last provision was aimed at weakening the power of colonial legislatures.

The Townsend duties went up for debate in June 1767. They were advertised as being "external" rather than "internal" taxes, an important distinction for many people. It was widely agreed that the duties would be accepted more readily than the Stamp Act, because they did not affect internal commerce in America. No less a personality than Franklin told parliament that Americans would not object to duties limited to imports. Franklin believed what he was saying, but in doing so he misled the British government.

The Revenue Act won quick approval in both houses of parliament, and George III gladly gave his consent to the measure. Everything was moving along smoothly until Townsend died unexpectedly just four months after the passage of his act. This left the chore of implementing his program to Lord Frederick North. North, even more convinced than

The Controversy Between Great Britain and Her Colonies

Published in 1769, *The Controversy Between Great Britain and Her Colonies Reviewed* painstakingly considers each and every colonial claim of British injustice and finds them hollow. Written by William Knox, a former agent for Georgia who worked in the Colonial Office in London, the pamphlet uses history, law, custom, and economic theory to challenge the colonists' prevailing notions concerning taxation and representation. According to Knox, the colonists' arguments are based on flawed knowledge and a gross misunderstanding of how imperial relationships function. Knox claims that if the Americans are correct about the liberties of British subjects, then the connection between them and the parent country are doomed. The author contends that American protests are clear evidence that the colonists and their counterparts in the parent country hold totally different ideas about the nature and extent of legitimate power. "What Englishman could desire more of the Colonies than due obedience to that august body, the parliament of Great Britain?" Knox asks. "But what is due obedience," he continues , "is a matter in which they and the people of England disagree exceedingly." Americans, in fact, define the term as meaning "no obedience at all."

William Knox, *The Controversy Between Great Britain and Her Colonies Reviewed.* London: J. Alnon, 1769; reprint, Boston: Old South Leaflets, p. 7.

Boston merchant John Hancock is shown in this engraving.

Townsend that America had to pay its own way, fully supported the goals of the Revenue Act. He promised the act's backers in parliament that "I will never think of repealing it, until I see America prostrate at my feet."[17]

Massachusetts—Again

News of the passage of the Townsend duties rekindled the flame of resistance that had smoldered in America for over a year. Once again Massachusetts took the lead. Meeting in a special session on

December 30, 1767, the Massachusetts House of Representatives drafted a letter to be sent to every other colony. This circular letter challenged parliament's right to tax Americans in any manner, internally or externally. The Revenue Act, the legislators wrote, was an infringement upon their "natural & Constitutional rights . . . because [Americans] are not represented in the British Parliament. . . . Being separated [from England] by an Ocean of a thousand leagues,"[18] Americans, Massachusetts argued, could only be represented in and taxed by their local assemblies. The New Englanders had said their piece and now asked to be heard by the other colonies.

Nothing in the circular letter was entirely new. Indeed, the Pennsylvania lawyer John Dickenson had already called into question the extent of parliament's authority in his widely read newspaper editorials *Letters from a Pennsylvania Farmer*. But the document drafted by Massachusetts was an official rejection of parliamentary power. As such, it generated an immediate British response. Most of the colonial assemblies were not in session when the circular letter arrived. Only three actually responded to it, but those legislatures—New Jersey, Connecticut, and Virginia—all agreed with its contents. It seemed unlikely that when the other legislatures convened they would think differently.

The circular letter expressed a popular opinion and promised to drum up resistance to the Townsend duties. In an effort to stop this from happening, the British government ordered Massachusetts to rescind, or call back, the letter. If the House of Representatives refused, Bernard was authorized to shut down the assembly and send the legislature home. Governors in the other colonies were similarly commanded to dissolve their legislatures if those bodies showed any support for Massachusetts or its letter.

Bernard did as he was told. Rescind or be sent home, he told the legislature. Led by Adams and James Otis Jr., both prominent Sons of Liberty, the House refused to take back its words on June 30, 1768, and was dissolved. By a margin of 92-17, Massachusetts had rejected the authority of Bernard and parliament in a single vote. The next day the *Boston Gazette* published the names of those who voted "no," enshrining them as the "Glorious Ninety-two."[19] When the governor received a written confirmation of the proceedings, he exclaimed, "Samuel Adams! Every dip of his pen stings like a horned snake."[20]

John Hancock's *Liberty*

While the politicians fought it out in the legislature, other Bostonians took a more physical approach. John Hancock was familiar in Boston not only as an outspoken radical but also as a respected and wealthy merchant. His money came from, among other things, trading in wine. It was wine that sat in the cargo hold of Hancock's trade ship *Liberty* when it entered Boston Harbor in May 1768 and unloaded its goods.

One month later the trouble began. The harbor official who had inspected the *Liberty* claimed to have been threatened if he ever revealed that its captain declared less cargo than the ship could hold, clear evidence of smuggling. Consequently, customs agents boarded and seized Hancock's sloop while a British warship stood by to protect them.

Noticing that the popular Hancock was having his property confiscated, a crowd gathered on the dock. The crowd became a mob and soon a riot broke out. The customs agents were attacked with clubs. Fires were set; windows were smashed all along the wharf. By the next morning several buildings were in ruins, and Boston seemed to be on the verge of anarchy. Bernard's response was prudent and predictable; the governor asked that troops be sent to restore order. As Hutchinson put it, "government must be aided from without or it must entirely subside and suffer anarchy to rise in its place."[21]

Harboring the same sentiment, Bernard asked General Thomas Gage, commander of British forces in America, for soldiers. Gage quickly approved the request. The general, notifying London of his decision, wrote that "the colonists are taking large strides towards independency." Regulars marching through the streets of Boston, Gage added, would show "that these colonies are British colonies . . . and they are not independent states."[22]

The as-yet unknown Paul Revere, a local silversmith, described the arrival of British soldiers late that September. As he stood on the dock, he watched as the warships tied up and disembarked the troops. Resplendent in their fine red-coated uniforms and shiny black boots, the men of the 14th and 29th infantry regiments, supported by a detachment of infantry from the 59th and an artillery company,

stepped ashore. Revere remarked with disgust on how the soldiers "Formed and Marched with insolent Parade . . . each soldier having received sixteen rounds of Powder and Ball."[23]

Trouble with the Lobsterbacks

The regulars did their best not to provoke the people of Boston. This was a challenge, given the fact that the troops were quartered in the city itself and not at Castle William in Boston harbor, as was customary. Complicating things further was the relentlessly hostile attitude of the townspeople. Hard looks and insults were commonly flung at the young soldiers, ridiculed as "lobsterbacks," sent to maintain order in unfriendly territory. Even local public officials took their turn in verbally abusing the royal troops. One Boston judge angrily challenged a group of soldiers he encountered on the street, saying, "Who brought you here? Who sent for you? . . . We want none of your guards. We have arms of our own, and can protect ourselves." He ended his tirade with an ominous warning: "You are but a handful. Better take care not to provoke us."[24]

The Bostonians generally despised the soldiers living among them. It did not help that some of the redcoats had black skin. Many of the drummers and standard bearers for the British regiments were black troops. These men came in for more than the usual amount of taunting and humiliation. Racism, as strong as any found in the American South, oozed on the streets of Boston. One elderly man felt so much hatred for the black soldiers in the king's service that he could not restrain himself when he passed by a black trooper. "You black rascal!" he exclaimed, "What have you to do with white people's quarrels?"[25] Like so many of his black royal soldiers, this unfortunate soldier had to let the insult pass.

Boycotts Begin

British troops and the townspeople in Boston eyed one another warily. Neither liked the other very much, and the distance between them only grew. Yet in terms of political advantage, the supporters of parliament's authority could certainly claim it. Colonial legislatures had been shut down or frightened into silence. Regular troops preserved law and order. The duties on import, most significantly the one placed on tea, were still in effect. British rule had been reinvigorated; American hopes had been frustrated. Only one course of action remained open to the colonists as they saw it—meet economic oppression with economic resistance. Drawing on experience gained during the Stamp Act crisis, a call went out from

The East India Company

Chartered in 1600, the East India Company was established in order to allow England to compete with France and the Netherlands for control of global trade. Its primary objective was to monopolize the lucrative trade in goods from India, namely spices, silk, cotton, gunpowder components, and tea. Like most English overseas ventures, the East India Company was a private firm that functioned as an extension of the royal government. It was, therefore, a key player in imperial political and economic affairs, as the 1773 Tea Act and subsequent controversy demonstrated. The company accumulated so much power in India that it dominated the subcontinent by 1757. The removal of the French after the treaty of 1763 and the later defeat of the independent Indian states only tightened the company's hold. By the mid-nineteenth century, it had also become known for its role in supplying opium to Chinese drug dealers, an activity that had the support of the British government. For all this, the company's heyday was somewhat brief. Following the disastrous mutiny of 1857, in which Indian soldiers hired by the company rose up in rebellion, the East India Company was dissolved. Its holdings in India were given up to the authorities in London, who initiated direct British administration.

Boston for a boycott of British-made goods. Merchants throughout the colonies were asked to pledge not to import or sell British products until the Townsend duties were lifted.

Again, as in 1765, the word "associations" hung on American lips. Merchants and manufacturers everywhere banded together in solidarity with their comrades in Boston. Businessmen from Massachusetts to Georgia refused to deal in British wares. Taking matters a step further, they announced their intention to shun anyone who did. Those who refused to join the boycott would be outcasts. The merchant association of Norwich, Connecticut, for example, declared openly that its members would boycott British goods and "avoid all correspondence with those merchants who shall dare violate these obligations."[26]

The response to the call for a boycott heartened the Sons of Liberty and other anti-parliament groups. Virginia planters agreed not to import slaves. Those in North Carolina did likewise. Colonial women and their daughters joined the movement, too. They promised not to serve British tea to their husbands. Women, with the primary responsibility for clothing American families, agreed to give up fancy dresses and sew only with "homespun" American cloth. Competing to prove the depth of their convictions, women and girls in one Massachusetts town produced an amazing 20,522 yards (18,765m) of homespun cloth in 1769 alone. In Lancaster, Pennsylvania, the women went one better; they wove 35,000 yards (32,000m). Together, Americans hoped to make their voices heard by hitting the British pocketbook.

A Tragedy in Boston

Parliament could not help but notice the boycott. London traders complained openly about cancelled orders and falling profits. Once more, parliament was forced to reconsider its decision to tax the Americans. Some prominent politicians quietly urged repeal, but support for the Townsend duties remained high in many circles. North, and those who thought as he did, refused to consider lifting the duties. He called for an even tougher reply to colonial stubbornness. "America must fear you," North claimed, "before she can love you. . . . I hope that we shall never think of [repeal]."[27] The prime minister and his supporters could think of no good reason to soften the hard line they had taken. They were about to get one.

British troops had been in Boston for almost two years by the late winter of 1770. During that time local men and soldiers had brawled in the taverns and on the streets. They had thrown horrible insults at one another, when their fists were not flying. Young Bostonians and young redcoats competed aggressively for part-time jobs and full-time relationships with the town's girls. Each day, each passing week and month, the tempers of both parties grew shorter. The threat of violence hung in the frigid air.

Finally, on March 5 the mutual hatred boiled over. Alone in front of the customs house on King Street, a British sentry was confronted by a group of drunken locals around 8:00 P.M. Within minutes a crowd

The Boston Massacre began on King Street in Boston on March 5, 1770.

began to gather. Soon snowballs and chunks of ice replaced the insults hurled by the mob. Emerging from the guard-house up the block, forty-year-old Captain Thomas Preston noticed his trooper backed up against the customs house door, brandishing his bayonet. Preston, as any officer would, called out the remainder of the guard to rescue the lone beleaguered sentry. In a moment six soldiers and a corporal were marching to the young guard's assistance. When they arrived they found themselves encircled by a swelling crowd, yelling profanities and now tossing stones as well as snowballs. One of the angry Bostonians called out to Preston, "I hope you do not intend they shall fire upon the inhabitants."[28] To

which Preston replied, "By no means, by no means."[29] A short time later, acrid gun smoke wafted over the street, and eleven citizens lay dead, dying, or wounded in the bloody snow.

Although Revere famously laid the blame on trigger-happy redcoats for the shootings in Boston, no one at the time knew for sure what had happened. The exact details of what came to be called the Boston Massacre were unclear. All anyone could say was that at some point a British musket discharged, leading the panicky soldiers to open fire on their tormentors. It was painfully apparent, though, that whatever the precise cause, the dispute over British authority had moved to a dangerous new level.

Hutchinson sensed that matters were spiraling out of control. In the immediate aftermath of the shootings, he had swiftly calmed Boston with promises of justice, promises of a trial. A trial was held with, of all people, Samuel Adams's cousin and fellow radical John Adams defending Preston and the soldiers accused of murder. Although he opposed British authority, Adams still supported the rule of law. He did an admirable job arguing the soldiers' case; Preston and all but two of his men were found not guilty. Those two soldiers were convicted of manslaughter, had their thumbs branded with a hot iron, and were released. No one, on either side, challenged the outcome of the trial. The shock of British soldiers shooting and killing British subjects was too severe. Everyone knew that the dispute over taxes and duties had taken a new and potentially explosive turn.

Another Repeal

The shootings in Boston finally persuaded even the most ardent supporters of a tough American policy to relent. Parliament began to cast about for a way to ease the growing tensions in the colonies without appearing to be weak. The Revenue Act had to go, but parliament's broader authority had to remain unquestioned. A com-

Crispus Attucks and Black America

One of the corpses lying in the snow on the night of March 5, 1770, was that of an escaped slave, Crispus Attucks. Before he died, Attucks was part of a black community that by 1770 had grown to around 21 percent of the total population in America. Almost all of these people were slaves. Yet, oppressed and marginalized as they were, many black Americans still actively participated in the Revolution. An estimated five thousand blacks joined the Continental army, most of them clustered in one of the army's three all-black regiments, such as the 1st Rhode Island. One German officer, who routinely encountered black Continentals, remarked that among troops from New England "you never see a regiment in which there are not negroes." Blacks fought alongside the redcoats in even greater numbers. As fighters, regiments such as Lord Dunmore's Ethiopian Regiment were feared by the rebels. The promise of freedom drew men to the colors in both cases. Unfortunately for these brave men, the war failed to change the status of most. That would have to await another far bloodier and more bitter conflict, the Civil War, to achieve.

Quoted in Sidney Kaplan and Emma Nogrady Kaplan, *The Black Presence in the Era of the American Revolution.* Amherst: University of Massachusetts Press, 1989, p. 34.

Samuel Adams was America's premier radical during the revolutionary period.

promise was arrived at after long and serious debate in the House of Commons. The Townsend duties would be repealed, with the exception of the duty on tea. The American Board of Customs Commissioners would remain at its post, and colonial officials would continue to be on the royal payroll. This partial repeal satisfied those Britons concerned with saving face and those stunned by the descent into bloodshed. It went into effect immediately.

For the next three years the uneasy calm was broken only by sporadic acts of defiance, limited almost exclusively to New England. The Sons of Liberty, by and large, went back to their daily lives. Only in Massachusetts was the flame of resistance tended closely. There, Hutchinson had replaced Bernard as governor, and Samuel Adams labored to hold the radical movement together by setting up town committees of correspondence. The committees' job was to keep people informed of government activities.

Here and there issues popped up that allowed Adams and the radicals to flex their muscles. But the British were careful to avoid doing anything to cause a resurgence of colonial anger. The radicals, as a result, could sense themselves slowly becoming irrelevant. Adams and other leaders in the movement needed some new issue to energize the colonists. They desperately needed some point of conflict around which to rally their distracted followers. They found that issue in a cup of tea.

A New Controversy

On May 10, 1773, parliament passed the Tea Act. Designed to revive the sagging fortunes of the British East India Company, the act ordered that customs duties would "be drawn back and allowed from all teas . . . [shipped] to any British

Tea

In the eighteenth century, as today, society was periodically swept by fads. One of these was tea, which surpassed chocolate and coffee as the English world's drink of choice. Only tobacco proved more popular as a consumer product. Mildly addictive, tea was wildly popular in England and more so in America. The tea drunk in the colonies came almost exclusively from British sources such as the East India Company. This combination of fashionable craving and imperial economics meant that disputes involving tea would spill over into a range of other issues. Tea was more than a hot, black, caffeinated drink; it was a symbol of the shared Englishness of people on both sides of the Atlantic. When Britain gave the East India Company a virtual monopoly on the tea trade, it convinced many Americans that parliament sought to imprison them in a teapot. Americans suddenly viewed a pleasing beverage as a tool of tyranny. This explains a popular cartoon at the time that portrays royal officials forcibly pouring tea down innocent America's throat. It also answers the question of tea's fall from favor during and after the Revolution.

colonies or plantations in America."[30] Put simply, the East India Company could route its tea shipments through English ports and sell it in America without paying a tax in both places. The British import duty would be paid by the government; Americans would continue to pay their tea tax through the existing duty collected at colonial ports.

Parliament never imagined that the Americans would rise up in protest against a piece of legislation that did not change their taxes at all. In fact, by lowering the costs to the East India Company, tea sold in America would be less expensive than before. Parliament certainly did not anticipate that it would be accused of trying to tyrannize the colonies. But that is what happened. The colonists saw in the Tea Act a monopoly for the East India Company and an unfair tax burden for themselves. Once more, Americans began talking of open resistance.

Chapter Three

A Rebellion in Massachusetts, 1773–1775

By the fall of 1773 tea ships were already under sail from England headed for America. Each one carried fresh shipments of the East India Company's black tea. Their destinations included the ports of New York, Charleston, Philadelphia, and Boston. For its part, Boston was scheduled to receive three vessels—the *Dartmouth*, the *Eleanor*, and the *Beaver*—all of which arrived safely in November 1773. Their captains had simple instructions: off-load the cases of tea in their holds, clear port, and return home for more. But nothing, it seemed, was simple in America, especially when it involved acts of parliament.

A Party in Boston Harbor

One by one, the tea ships came in. No sooner had the *Dartmouth* dropped anchor than an anti–Tea Act riot broke out, leaving the captain unable to deposit his cargo. The Sons of Liberty also organized welcoming committees for the *Eleanor* and the *Beaver*, physically preventing them from putting their tea ashore.

With the ships moored but still loaded, Samuel Adams and the radicals went to work. Speaking before a packed town meeting held at the Old South Meeting House, Adams railed against the Tea Act and urged his fellow Bostonians to reject Britain's offer of this "shameful luxury." He said to the assembled audience, "We are duty bound to use our most strenuous endeavors to ward off the impending evil, and we are sure that, upon a fair and cool inquiry . . . you will think this tea now coming to us to be more dreaded than plague or pestilence." Adams concluded by exhorting his listeners to "rise and resist this and every other plan for our destruction."[31] The radical message proved so convincing that the crowd voted almost unanimously to have "the tea . . . returned to the place from whence it came, at all events."[32]

This lithograph depicts the Boston Tea Party. Ninety thousand pounds of tea were thrown into the water.

Even an appeal directly from the *Dartmouth*'s owner, an American himself, did no good. Francis Rotch traveled to Boston and pleaded with the radicals. The customs collector had informed Rotch that if his ship tried to clear port without landing its cargo, the royal navy stood by to seize the vessel. Caught in the middle, Rotch begged Adams to let the tea come ashore. Adams stubbornly replied that "the ship must go. The people of Boston and neighboring towns absolutely require and expect it."[33]

Nearly a week later the stalemate ended in dramatic fashion. On the night of December 16, 1773, a party of men disguised as Indians slipped aboard the tea ships. The raiders overpowered the crews, opened the holds, and lifted case after case of tea up to the decks. There, with swift ax blows, the chests were chopped apart, and the contents were spilled overboard. Jubilant at the destruction, a young "Indian" exclaimed, "What a cup of tea we're making for the fishes."[34] Another one of the culprits, questioned by his wife, told her that he had been out with his friends "making a little saltwater tea."[35] On their way back home through the streets of Boston, the men were treated to the cheers and applause of onlookers. The total amount of damage done that night was impressive: Ninety thousand pounds of tea had gone into the water, valued at approximately $1 million in today's currency.

Parliament's Turn

The dumping of the tea marked the end of parliament's patience with the American colonies, Massachusetts most of all. Furious at American defiance of its power and the destruction of valuable private property, parliament decided to crack down. Boston, viewed by many Britons as a nest of agitators and traitors, would be made to feel the full effect of the government's might. All of Massachusetts, in fact, would be taught a lesson in proper obedience to the king's administration.

"Whereas dangerous commotions and insurrections have been fomented and raised in the town of Boston,"[36] parliament declared in March 1774, its harbor was officially closed to all traffic. After a three-month grace period, nothing would be permitted to enter or leave the port. The next blow fell in May. The Massachusetts House of Representatives was stripped of its power to appoint colonial officials, including councilors, judges, justices of the peace, and sheriffs. The royal governor would now make those appointments, and the new royal

Immigration and Ideology

Early on, most immigrants to America came from England, but by the Revolutionary era that had changed. Almost one hundred and fifty thousand Scots-Irish had reached America by 1760, nearly all of whom settled on the frontier. Seventy-five thousand Germans had arrived by the same date, concentrating themselves in farm communities in Pennsylvania and New Jersey. More than one hundred and seventy-five thousand slaves also arrived. These unwilling immigrants, for the most part, were forced to live in the South. Between 1760 and 1775, immigration continued—fifty-five thousand Irish Protestants, forty thousand Scots, and thirty thousand English crossed the Atlantic to add their numbers to a growing population. These groups went their own ways. The Irish and Scots joined their ethnic cousins on the frontier; the newly arrived English clustered in the cities. In terms of support for the rebel cause, a trend emerged that even people at the time recognized: Fresh immigrants and frontier folk tended toward loyalism; older residents in cities and farmers leaned toward rebellion. Recent immigrants, it seems, did not feel much connection to their better-established American neighbors; new arrivals living on the frontier trusted distant royal authority more than that of the local colonial political elite. Slaves' loyalties were determined by their masters' wishes or offers of freedom.

Quoted in Charles Royster, *A Revolutionary People at War: The Continental Army and American Character, 1775–1783.* New York: W.W. Norton, 1979, p. 41.

governor was Gage, a military man. Town meetings, always a favored venue for radical spokesmen, were prohibited, except for one meeting each year at the governor's discretion. The Boston Port Bill and the Massachusetts Governance Act were two of what the colonists called the "Intolerable Acts."

When word reached them about what was going on, the other colonies reacted first with shock and then with anger. Virginia, for instance, set June 1, the day the Port Act was scheduled to go into effect, as a day of prayer and support for its "sister colony." The Virginia Assembly asked the colony's people to ask God to help them avoid "the heavy calamity which threatens destruction to our civil rights, and the evils of civil war."[37] Virginia's royal governor, Lord Dunmore, promptly closed the assembly hall, leaving its delegates with no place to meet except a local tavern. There they called for another colonial congress, this time a Continental Congress, to address what was now imagined to be a general assault on American freedom.

The First Continental Congress

Word of the proposed congress spread quickly. Reviving the committees of correspondence as messengers, radical leaders called for delegations from each colony to converge on Philadelphia. By September 5, 1774, fifty-five men from twelve colonies were ready to discuss what action could be taken to support Massachusetts and protect their own liberties. Only Georgia, taking a wait-and-see attitude, failed to send a representative.

By and large, the men who met at Philadelphia were an unimpressive lot. John Adams remarked that it was a shame that America could not produce better leaders. "We have not men fit for the times,"[38] Adams lamented. The only name uttered at the meeting that drew any notice at all was that of an obscure Virginia militia colonel. This man gained attention when he offered to "raise one thousand men [and] march myself at their head for the relief of Boston."[39] His name was George Washington.

A Threat and an Association

The congress got down to business without much delay. After some debate the delegates said that if parliament did not repeal the Intolerable Acts by December 1, 1774, Americans would begin boycotting British goods. If the legislation was not erased by September 30, 1775, the colonists would no longer export goods either.

Effective immediately, the congress also ordered Americans not to consume any product made in Britain. Committees of inspection would ensure that everyone did as the congress wanted, or else. "Any person," deemed not in compliance with this new Continental Association, it was ordered, "would be universally condemned as the enemies of American liberty." In other words, anyone who chose not to support the radical agenda could expect their one-time friends and neighbors to "break off all dealings with him or her."[40]

Patrick Henry addresses the First Continental Congress in Philadelphia in 1774.

The Massachusetts Revolution Begins

The First Continental Congress adjourned on October 24, agreeing to meet again the following May. Meanwhile, the Massachusetts assembly had come back together, illegally, in the town of Concord. It now called itself the Massachusetts Provincial Congress and claimed power. Acting the part of a legitimate government, the provincial congress assumed authority over the Massachusetts militia, reorganized it, and put it under the control of a committee for public safety. This commit-

tee then set up special fifty-man units, known as "minute companies," which were to be ready to fight the British regulars at a minute's notice. It also confiscated guns and ammunition from militia stores and authorized the formation of a network of spies to report on British activity inside Boston. One of the spy-masters was the silversmith Revere.

By December 1774 royal patience had run out. George III declared the colony of Massachusetts to be in a state of rebellion. "Blows must decide," he told North, "whether they are to be subject to this

General Thomas Gage, commander of British forces in America, is shown here.

tiamen, including Washington, during the Seven Years' War. Gage knew the country and its people—and he did not like Boston. "America is a mere bully," he once remarked, "and the Bostonians are by far the greatest bullies."[42]

Gage planned to deal harshly with these bullies. He had been given the authority to arrest the leaders of the provincial congress, chief among them Adams and Hancock, as a logical first step in bringing Massachusetts to heel. Gage, however, had to plot the arrests carefully. Taking prominent organizers into custody would not be enough. Gage knew that he would also have to seize the arms and ammunition belonging to the rebel militias. In the recent past, just the rumor of royal troops moving against the militias had been sufficient to put the countryside in arms. These so-called powder alarms had convinced Gage that a cautious approach was the best one.

"One if by Land, Two if by Sea"

After a good deal of thinking and planning, Gage finally moved against the rebellion. Undercover agents had given him the precise location of Adams and Hancock. They had also provided him with maps and other intelligence about the countryside. Gage discovered that the two leaders were in Lexington but would soon be in Concord, where the provincial congress was meeting. Concord also held a large store of weapons that included muskets, ammunition, gunpowder, and even a few cannons. This small town on the banks of a slow-moving river, then, would be his target. The preparations began.

Country or independent."[41] Accordingly, he authorized Gage to take all necessary measures to restore order in New England. Someone had to put matters straight, and he was that person. George III, North, and the current secretary for American affairs, Lord Dartmouth, all felt Gage to be the right man for the job. He was married to an American, he owned land in New York, and he had fought alongside colonial mili-

Gage's efforts were hardly a secret. Everyone in Boston could sense that something was going on, especially Revere and his network of spies. They watched as British troops in Boston shifted their positions all through early April 1775. The real question was Gage's route to Concord. Two possible approaches were open to the British. One was straight out of town along the peninsula called the Boston Neck. The other began in Charlestown and required crossing a river beforehand. The road chosen by the British would determine the position of any militia blocking force, so it was important to know which one Gage wanted to use.

Paul Revere's famous ride occurred on April 18, 1775.

Revere, therefore, decided that as soon as it became certain how the British would get to Concord, a secret message would be sent to the appropriate militia companies. If the regulars chose to march out along the Neck, one lamp would be hung in the steeple of Boston's Old North Church. If they chose to cross the Charles River before hitting the road to Concord, two lamps would be lit and hung for the rebels to see. Revere himself volunteered to ride out, under cover of darkness, and alert the rebel leadership while the militia got ready to oppose Gage's force.

Paul Revere's Ride

On the night of Tuesday, April 18, 1775, the British intentions were finally revealed. The elite troops assembled by Gage began loading into boats along the banks of the Charles. They carried supplies for a few days in the field. Revere had two lamps lifted to the top of the Old North Church and quietly slipped across to Charlestown.

The Battle of Lexington is depicted in this painting.

The Minuteman Myth

As the provincial congress moved to become Massachusetts's revolutionary government in 1774, it necessarily assumed control of and reorganized the colony's militia. The result was a two-tiered military structure that included both regular units and so-called "minute companies." Although imagined today to have implied some sort of elite status, the name had nothing to do with skill level or degree of preparedness. Militias in the eighteenth century kept their weapons and ammunition in local armories overseen by committees composed of senior militia officers. The colonial governments closely regulated these storage facilities. When trouble arose, militiamen went to their armory, drew their muskets and a prescribed quantity of powder and shot, and formed up on the village green. After the alarm had passed, the weapons and ammunition went back into storage. The only difference with minute companies was that their members were allowed to keep their firearms and ammunition at home. This reduced the response time during a crisis. Minutemen might have reacted more quickly, but that did not make them better soldiers. "As to the Minute Men," General Charles Lee complained, "no account ought to be made of them."

From there, he "immediately set off for Lexington, where . . . Hancock and Adams were [to tell] them of the movement and it was thought they were the objects."[43] Revere rode hard, dodging British patrols and rousing militiamen along the way.

He finally arrived at the Lexington house where Hancock and Adams were staying and demanded to see them. The guard responded by telling Revere to keep down the noise; the rebel leaders were sleeping. "Noise!" Revere yelled, "You'll have noise before long. The regulars are coming out!"[44] At that, he was allowed to deliver his message. Hancock and Adams made their escape. Revere rode out to alert Concord's defenders.

Lexington Green

As Revere galloped away, Lexington's militia formed up on the village green, prepared to protect the town and block the British column headed for Concord. The British troops, led by the incompetent Colonel Francis Smith but actually commanded by the far more capable marine major John Pitcairn, were not seeking a fight this early in their mission. Still, being well-trained and well-disciplined men, they would not avoid one if the Americans got in their way at Lexington.

By this time Revere and two riding companions, William Dawes and Samuel Prescott, had been intercepted by a British reconnaissance party. Dawes and Prescott escaped, but Revere did not. Eventually, the soldiers released him but not before being told by Revere that the whole countryside had been alerted to their presence. The British horsemen let Revere go, as he knew they would, and rode hard to inform Smith.

Told that his operation had been discovered, Smith sent word to Boston requesting reinforcements and pushed onward. At 5:00 a.m. the British arrived in Lexington to find Hancock and Adams gone and Captain John Parker's seventy-five militiamen arrayed on the village green. The regulars neatly formed a skirmish line opposite the Americans, as they had been trained to do. Pitcairn rode forward and ordered the armed townsmen to go home. "Disperse you villains, you rebels! Disperse! Lay down your arms!"[45] he commanded. At first, the militiamen seemed ready to comply, but then a musket shot cracked the air. No one was sure who fired it, but the regulars responded as any soldiers would—they opened fire. Within minutes, the green was cleared of defenders. Eight Americans had died in the first battle of the American Revolution.

Concord and the Long Road Back

The British drums began to beat as the column moved out of Lexington. Smith and Pitcairn rode confidently at its head, unaware that Prescott had already warned Concord of their intentions. By the time the regulars arrived, at about 8:00 A.M., the militia had pulled out and reassembled in the hills surrounding the town. Unopposed, the British set about destroying any arms they could find and making a halfhearted effort to find any stray provincial congressmen. They set up defensive positions along the Concord River and secured the North Bridge.

It was at this same North Bridge that the British came under attack for the first time from a sizable American force. Reinforced by their comrades from neighboring towns, the Concord men fought a British scouting party and pushed it backward. At the bridge itself, a confused battle ensued. Neither side really had the advantage or inflicted a great deal of damage on the other. One American recalled of the British marksmen, "their [musket] balls whistled well . . . but they fired too high."[46] The militiamen had trouble hitting their targets as well. Nevertheless, Smith thought it best to evacuate Concord and lead his men back to Boston. A relief column had already been dispatched by Gage to meet them along the way.

Until that point it would not be an easy return trip. The Americans took up positions along the road and peppered Smith's regiment with continuous fire. A British lieutenant remembered how the regulars were "fired upon from all sides, but mostly from the rear, where people hid in houses till we passed."[47] Another redcoat told how "the Rebels kept up an incessant irregular fire from all points on the column . . . they hardly ever fired but under cover of some stone wall, from behind a tree, or out of a house."[48]

This is a reproduction of the Old North Bridge where the colonial Minutemen fought the British on April 19, 1775.

Suffering under ferocious musket fire, the British soldiers maintained their order and kept marching. Their officers demonstrated their courage as well. While directing return shots, Pitcairn calmly selected men to sweep out to the sides of the column and clear adjacent houses of rebel snipers. They completed their mission quickly and ruthlessly, using bayonets to silently dispatch their enemies. House by house, stone wall by stone wall, tree by tree, the road to Boston was fought over.

By midday Smith's regiment had linked up with a relief column led by Brigadier general Hugh Lord Percy. Percy's unit covered Smith's retreat by pouring cannon fire into the Americans. Not being real soldiers, the Americans were unable to face artillery. They broke off the pursuit and fled. The British force withdrew into Boston under the protection of the fortifications Gage had set up. They were safe but battered.

Gage praised Smith, Pitcairn, and Percy in his report to London. In his opinion, they "did everything men could do, as did all the officers in general, and the men behaved with their usual intrepidity."[49] There was certainly no shortage of valor and sacrifice on the journey back from Concord. The British soldiers had fought well, but they were also now surrounded

The British Edge

On the eve of the Revolution the British army was the best-trained, best-equipped, and most ably led fighting force in the world. No other army had experienced such success on the battlefield; no other army was more respected. The record of victory compiled by the redcoats resulted in many different advantages, one being raw firepower. For instance, the average soldier's skill with the .75-caliber smoothbore musket, nicknamed the "Brown Bess," proved decisive in battle after battle. Accurate to 75 yards (68.6m) but able to hit a man-sized target at 100 yards (91.4m), the "Brown Bess" was lethal in trained hands. During volley fire, the British musket could devastate an enemy. Faster to reload and easier to maintain than a rifled musket and more durable than other European smoothbores, it was a versatile weapon, too. When tipped with a 15- to 30-inch bayonet (38cm to 76cm), the gun was transformed into a terrifying and deadly close-quarters combat tool. More than one American unit during the Revolution broke and ran at the mere sight of rows of redcoats, their nut-brown muskets sporting gleaming bayonets. In a multitude of ways, the British Army was a formidable opponent for the Continentals.

by an ever-growing number of militia companies from throughout New England. Soon these units would be joined by their comrades from other colonies. Drawn by news of the "victory" over the hated lobsterbacks and the prospect of fighting against what they believed was a challenge to their liberty, American men gathered around Boston. The war had begun; Boston was besieged. The Massachusetts rebellion now became an American revolution.

Chapter Four

Victory, Defeat, and a Declaration, 1775–1776

Gage, in the spring of 1775, sat uneasily in Boston as American militiamen milled about outside the city. For all intents and purposes, he was trapped. Every day more rebels took up positions around him. North and Lord George Germain, the recently appointed secretary for American affairs, soon learned of Gage's predicament. They decided, after some discussion, that Gage was not up to the job of handling matters on his own. He needed help, they agreed, so they sent Major general Sir William Howe, Major general Sir Henry Clinton, and Major general Sir John Burgoyne to join him.

Gage, always sensitive about his authority, welcomed his new colleagues coolly. He knew already that one of them would likely be his replacement if the situation in America became any worse. Unless Gage could regain control of at least Massachusetts, he would surely be relieved. He had to act and act decisively.

The Second Continental Congress

While Gage pondered his choices, his opponents formally took action to make the Massachusetts rebellion an intercolonial effort. Reconvening on May 10, 1775, the Continental Congress faced an agenda full of important issues. At the top of the list was the fighting in New England. The armed resistance against the British was spreading outward from Boston. Everywhere, people seemed to be picking up muskets to oppose imperial authority. British forts in northern New York had been captured by rebel militiamen, taking the fighting to the Canadian border. In Pennsylvania rebel sympathizers defied their Quaker colony's reputation for nonviolence and called for the militia to take the field "for the Purpose of defending with Arms, their Property, Liberty, and Lives against all Attempts to deprive them." [50] Three militia battalions, along with cavalry and artillery companies,

George Washington takes command of the Continental Army at Cambridge on July 3, 1775.

marched through the streets of Philadelphia itself to show support for their comrades in Massachusetts. Throughout the South, rebel groups prepared to do battle with their loyalist neighbors.

No one at the congress doubted that a revolution was beginning, nor did they have any illusions about the British response. Gage would certainly counterattack, and parliament had already begun the process of reinforcing the army in the colonies. Full-scale war was coming, and that required a full-scale American army. In order to create just that kind of organization, the congress officially adopted the force around Boston, christening it the Continental army. The delegates, to demonstrate colonial unity, authorized the raising of rifle companies in Pennsylvania, Maryland, and Virginia. These troops would move north and make the war a common effort. Shared danger and shared sacrifice would unite Americans. To further stitch the North and South together, Congress chose a Virginian as Continental commander in chief. George Washington was given command of "all the continental forces, raised, or to be raised, for the defense of American liberty."[51]

The Battle of Bunker Hill

Washington quickly began formulating a plan to put the American army into fighting shape. He knew that speed was essential. Washington had to get to Massachusetts and get his new army ready to do battle against the best military force in the world. More immediately, he had to make sure that the British did not try to break out of Boston. Gage, however, did not wait for him.

Two days after Congress selected Washington to lead the American troops, Gage tried to punch through the siege lines around Boston. After consulting with his new "advisers"—Howe, Clinton, and Burgoyne—Gage decided to send Howe across the Charles River in force and smash the Americans, who had entrenched themselves along Breed's Hill. Bunker Hill, the initial choice for a defensive line, was decided to be too far from the anticipated landing beach, so the troops dug in on Breed's Hill.

At 3:30 A.M. on June 17, 1775, Howe and a contingent of nearly fifteen hundred men stepped off his boats. Three charges later he had cleared the Americans off of Breed's Hill, but at a frightful cost. Two hundred and twenty-six British soldiers lay dead in the grass; 828 more were wounded, many severely. American losses amounted to 140 dead and 271 wounded. Clinton, who had never really

The Battle of Bunker Hill cost hundreds of British and American lives.

supported Gage's decision to attack across the Charles River, said later that what became known as the Battle of Bunker Hill was a "dear bought victory, another such would have ruined us."[52] A junior officer serving with Howe's force was a bit more blunt. "The brave men's lives were thrown away," he fumed. "[Gage] as much murdered them as if he had cut their throats himself."[53]

Gage, it was said, had won a battle that should not have been fought and taken losses he had not needed to take.

Back home in Britain the general's victory was seen as a defeat. Parliament promptly relieved Gage of command and replaced him with Howe, who would share his responsibilities, and authority, with Clinton and Burgoyne. Meanwhile, outside Boston, Washington arrived on July 2 to take over operations for the Americans.

Canada

As the tall Virginian and his men settled in around Boston, an ambitious and dar-

A monument at Bunker Hill commemorates the first major battle of the Revolutionary War.

ing scheme took shape in Philadelphia. The Continental Congress decided to try a novel path to victory, one that involved both combat and diplomacy. On July 15 the delegates issued the Olive Branch Petition, asking George III to break off hostilities and start negotiating a settlement that would satisfy the Americans. Simultaneously, the congress authorized an invasion of Canada. The plan was to capture the cities of Montreal and Quebec, bringing the Canadians into a forced union with the rebellious colonies. The Canadian campaign would have two prongs. General Richard Montgomery would take Montreal, while Colonel Benedict Arnold was assigned the job of capturing Quebec after a grueling overland journey through the frozen woods of Maine. The two prongs would meet at Quebec, and Canada would belong to the Continental Congress.

Or so it was supposed to go. In actuality, the campaign turned into a disaster. Montgomery took Montreal, and he and Arnold linked up at Quebec as planned. Arnold's men, however, had been worn down by the march north, and Montgomery was killed soon after his arrival. Arnold himself fell ill and could barely direct the assault on the city. Worse still, the local support that had been hoped for failed to materialize. Rather than rising up to aid the rebels from the thirteen colonies, Canadians rallied to the king. Despite boasting that he had "no thought of leaving the proud town, until I first enter it in triumph,"[54] Arnold was compelled to break off the siege of Quebec and retreat back to New England. Canada remained solidly British.

The first page of the Olive Branch Petition sent by the First Contintental Congress to King George III is shown.

The Revolution Becomes Official

As the invasion of Canada was getting underway, the congress received word that George III had refused even to look at the Olive Branch Petition. Instead, he flew into a blind rage at the mere thought of negotiating with men he considered to be criminals. On August 23, 1775, the king formally declared America to be in "an open and avowed Rebellion." He furthermore ordered his government "to

King Louis XVI of France gave financial aid to the Americans.

Augustin, Caron de Beaumarchais, the three agents were introduced to Charles Gravier, Comte de Vergennes, chief minister to the French monarch. Vergennes hated the British and saw support for the Americans as a critical first step in regaining for France what it had lost in 1763. Secret negotiations began soon afterward.

Good News and Bad News in the Spring of 1776

The congress learned of Arnold's repulse at Quebec around the same time that it was informed that parliament had passed a Prohibitory Act effectively cutting off American trade. The congress also found out that the king had begun hiring German mercenaries for his army in America. The only good news came from Washington.

The siege of Boston had forced Howe to evacuate the city. Washington's army had acquired cannons from the recently captured British Fort Ticonderoga. With these artillery pieces the Americans could now pound the garrison in Boston from the hills to the south. Howe could not break out, and now he could not stay put. Evacuation was his only option. Packing his belongings, Howe put his men and as many loyal Americans as he could on transport ships. The last one left Boston harbor on March 17, 1776. The cradle of the rebellion fell back into American hands.

The evacuation of Boston lifted spirits in Philadelphia considerably. Howe's departure removed the largest single British force from colonial soil. Even better was the news in May that Louis XVI

suppress such Rebellion, and to bring the Traitors to Justice."[55] The Americans were now outlaws.

Advised of their new status, the men at Philadelphia decided to make the most of it. The congress sent Arnold and Montgomery northward and agents abroad. Three men in particular were assigned the task of acquiring secret foreign aid for the rebellion. Arthur Lee, Silas Deane, and Benjamin Franklin were ordered to Paris. Their job was to seek out a sympathetic and well-connected Frenchman willing to convince King Louis XVI to give money and guns to the Americans. Through the services of a playwright named Pierre

had authorized the transfer of guns and ammunition to the rebels. France had nursed a grudge against Britain since the Seven Years' War. Aiding the rebellion would hurt the British and possibly lead to a return of some of the territory lost after France's defeat. A secret agreement with the Americans, therefore, proved too attractive to pass up. The French king allowed Beaumarchais and Vergennes to create a fictitious company, Rodrigue Hortalez et Compagnie, to funnel munitions to the colonies. Cash soon followed. Congress suddenly had two things it desperately needed—money and guns.

French arms proved crucial in the years to come. More than one commentator has agreed with the writer Robert Harvey's conclusion that "without French arms supplies the American war effort would probably have collapsed in 1776."[56] The twin blows of the king's rejection of peace and the failed Canadian expedition were softened considerably by Howe's retreat and the French deal. The relief felt by many on the rebel side, however, did not last long. A moment of decision was fast approaching that would set the rebellion on the road to total success or complete failure.

Free and Independent States

During that first winter of rebellion, 1775–1776, a recently arrived immigrant from England wrote one of the most

General Howe evacuates Boston in early 1776, removing the largest single British force from colonial soil.

German Mercenaries

As the fighting in America expanded in 1775, King George III augmented his forces by recruiting German mercenaries, soldiers who fought for pay alone. Getting these soldiers was easy to do because the king was still technically from the German noble family of Hanover. Being a member of the House of Hanover, he had the ability to hire thirty thousand troops from six different German states. Most of the men came from Brunswick, but a good number came from Hesse. Americans, not knowing the exact origins of the Germans, called all of them Hessians. Some of the mercenaries were used to protect British possessions in Europe, but the majority went to America. There they fought in several key battles and served as garrison troops in areas securely under British control. German assistance proved useful to the British but ultimately counterproductive. The employment of paid soldiers, renowned for their brutality, turned many potential loyalists against the crown. They were disappointed that their king would send foreign "hirelings," who saw all Americans as the enemy, to settle a dispute between Englishmen. Historians generally feel that using German mercenaries to fight Americans hurt more than it helped the British cause.

important political essays in American history. Born in England in 1737, Thomas Paine arrived in the colonies in late 1774. He immediately fell in with a group of radicals who believed that only independence could solve America's problems. Over time, Paine himself came to feel strongly that the colonies would be better off as independent states. He expressed that belief most clearly and convincingly in his January 1776 essay "Common Sense."

Published in pamphlet form, "Common Sense" sold over one hundred thousand copies in its first year alone. The piece's radical message resonated with a sizable number of American readers. "Government even in its best state," Paine wrote, "is but a necessary evil; in its worst state an intolerable one."[57] That, in Paine's opinion, was the current condition of the imperial government—intolerable. Great Britain had become corrupt and vicious. The parent country had turned on its own colonies, Paine argued, and "even brutes do not devour their own young, nor savages make war upon their families."[58] Parliament and the king together had committed both sins. Paine concluded, therefore, that the "blood of the slain, the weeping voice of nature cries, 'TIS TIME TO PART.'"[59] Freedom could now come only from independence, he said.

The process of divorce began on May 15, 1776, when Virginia authorized its representatives in Philadelphia to propose independence to the congress. Less than a month later Virginia's Richard Henry Lee asked his colleagues to agree that the colonies "are, and of right ought to be, free and independent states." In recognition of that fact, Lee continued, "all political connection between them and the State of Great Britain is, and ought to be, totally dissolved."[60] Most of the delegates agreed, so Thomas Jefferson, John Adams, Benjamin Franklin, Roger Sherman, and Robert Livingston were directed to write arguably the most revolutionary document the world had ever seen. On July 2 the congress held a preliminary vote on independence. Referring to the declaration produced by the committee, nine out of the thirteen delegations voted for immediate separation. Two, South Carolina and Pennsylvania, voted against it; Delaware was split; and New York abstained.

Although not yet unanimous, John Adams was thrilled by the results of the vote. He wrote to his wife Abigail that the "second day of July 1776, will be the most memorable in the history of America."[61] Adams confidently predicted that future generations would celebrate July 2 with festivities and fireworks. As it turned out, he was off by only two days. On July 4, 1776, twelve of the thirteen delegations agreed to independence, and the United States of America was created. It would be another year before the Articles of Confederation would organize and give legal structure to the new American government, but the deed was done. Now all the young republic had to do was to survive. That would be the hard part.

Howe Strikes

Since the evacuation of Boston, Washington had been trying to guess where and when his adversary might return. Anyplace along the coast, from Massachusetts to Georgia, could be the target. The most

This is the title page from "Common Sense" by Thomas Paine.

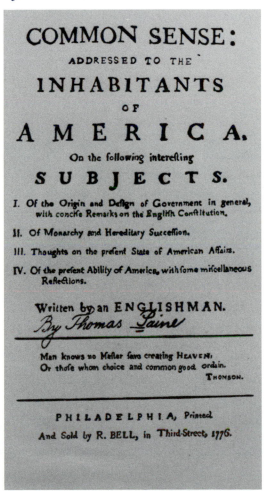

obvious landing points, however, were near the major port cities, chief among them New York. A landing there would put Howe in effective control of an important harbor at the mouth of the Hudson River. British control of the Hudson would cut off New England from the rest of America. The British could then attack the two parts in turn. Washington, aware of all this, moved his growing army to New York. His guess was correct. Howe had indeed decided to retake America through a New York–Hudson River strategy. The general felt certain that victory there would mean the end of the rebellion.

In June 1776 Howe's invasion force left Nova Scotia. It was made up of 30 war-ships and 170 transports carrying 40,000 troops, 8,000 of whom were German mercenaries. After floating at anchor for a few days off the New Jersey shore, the armada entered New York harbor and occupied Staten Island on July 3, the day before Congress declared independence.

Washington nervously followed the developments. As Howe landed his men, Washington conferred with his staff, which included perhaps the finest officer in the army, General Charles Lee. Lee, an experienced and aggressive leader, agreed with Washington that the defense of New York City was not possible on Manhattan. The best place to meet Howe would be across the East River on Long

This painting depicts the signing of the Declaration of Independence.

General Howe and his troops parade through New York as they take over the city during the American War of Independence.

Island. That is where Washington decided to give battle.

Howe gave it to him. On August 22 Howe's ships put ashore a strike force of fifteen hundred troops near modern-day Brooklyn, southeast of the American front lines. Washington told his army to fight "like men, like soldiers, for all that is worth living for is at stake."[62] His words of encouragement did little good. Soon after the British began their attack, Washington watched in horror as his line buckled and broke. Surprised by the appearance of British soldiers on their flank, the Americans collapsed. As one of Washington's men recalled, "The main body of the British, by a route we never dreamed of, had surrounded us, and driven within the lines or scattered in the woods, all our men."[63] Washington knew that he could not hold Long Island and could not defend New York City. The only alternative was to fall back, keeping one step ahead of Howe.

Retreat to New Jersey

Through sheer luck, a little fog, and the exertions of men from Massachusetts who had experience working boats, Washington withdrew to Manhattan on August 30. He had with him nine thousand tired, beaten men. Howe controlled

Nature's God: Religion and the Revolution

Religion played a major role in the Revolution. Ministers, especially those from New England, generated revolutionary fervor before the war and helped maintain it through the toughest times during the fighting. Although some churchmen urged their congregations to remain loyal to Britain, most did not. They generally portrayed America as a new Israel, fighting its way out of captivity. Americans had long imagined themselves to be on a divine mission to carve a promised land out of the wilderness. The revolution only amplified that sense of purpose. Ministers told their people that the rebel cause was a righteous one, a battle for liberty that had God's approval. Led by Congregationalists, Baptists, Methodists, and Presbyterians, but including other denominations, churches served, according to historian Edwin S. Gaustad, as "a social, cultural, and political force of unrivalled power" during the Revolution. It is little wonder that Thomas Jefferson, in the Declaration of Independence, felt compelled to appeal not only to "the opinions of mankind" as he justified the rebellion, but also to "Nature's God."

Edwin S. Gaustad, "Religion Before the Revolution," in *The Blackwell Encyclopedia of the American Revolution*, eds. Jack P. Greene and J.R. Pole. Cambridge, MA: Basil Blackwell, 1991, p. 69.

Long Island, while warships commanded by his brother Admiral Richard Howe ruled the East River. Making a stand on Manhattan would have spelled utter catastrophe for the American army and cause. So, Washington kept moving. He evacuated New York and retreated toward New Jersey, narrowly escaping several British attempts to corner him.

Along the way the casualties and bad news mounted. Each engagement with the British cost Washington dearly in terms of men killed, wounded, and captured. By November the shrinking Continental army had crossed the Hudson River and was racing south through the sandy pine forests of New Jersey. Behind Washington lay not only the bodies of many of his men but also the ruins of two forts captured by Howe's British and German troops. The American commander had also lost Charles Lee, who was taken prisoner as he slept in a room at a New Jersey tavern.

Washington's army now numbered a mere three thousand men, and new recruits were becoming scarce. These truly were desperate days, as Thomas Paine, who had joined the army, wrote in his essay "The American Crisis." "These are the times that try men's souls," Paine lamented. "The summer soldier and the sunshine patriot will, in this crisis, shrink from the service of their country."[64] The

New Jersey summer had long since turned to fall. The air was cold; snow was not far off. Pursued now by Howe's most able assistant, General Charles Lord Cornwallis, Washington pushed on toward Pennsylvania. The war, it seemed, might end sooner than anyone had imagined.

A Christmas in Trenton

Howe certainly felt confident of victory. So much so that in addition to hunting down the remnants of Washington's army, he opened peace talks with American representatives. Meeting with John Adams and Benjamin Franklin in New York, Howe asked them to convey to the congress his terms for surrender. Both men refused. The British had to go home, Adams and Franklin said firmly, and give the colonies their freedom. There the brief negotiations ended, and with them any hope for a diplomatic solution. Matters would be resolved on the battlefield. As one writer has noted, with the failure of the talks, "the war remained George Washington's to lose or win."[65]

Washington, for his part, was determined not to lose, at least not yet. After crossing the ice-choked Delaware River into Pennsylvania in early December, Washington doubled back. In a nighttime assault on Christmas Eve, 1776, he

George Washington's December 24, 1776, surprise attack on the British post in Trenton, New Jersey, proved successful.

attacked the German-manned British outpost at Trenton, New Jersey. The Americans defeated the sleepy, drunken Germans, and quickly captured several other small garrisons. Washington even succeeded in stalling the advance of British reinforcements at the Battle of Princeton on January 3, 1777. His men, however, were too worn out and short of vital supplies to go on. Having proven that he still had some fight left in him, Washington took his army into winter quarters at Morristown, New Jersey. Howe decided to spend the winter enjoying the pleasures of New York and left the Americans alone, for the time being. The year that had just ended had witnessed the bright hope of independence darkened by military defeat. No one was quite sure what 1777 held in store for the Americans and their revolution.

Chapter Five

South from Saratoga, 1777–1779

Washington had been defeated in 1776, but Howe had not been victorious. As long as the rebellion remained active and Washington remained in the field commanding troops, true victory eluded the British. More decisive action was required than Howe had taken to date. A new plan was needed, a plan not just to beat Washington but one to win the war. Indeed, a gamble would have to be taken on a strategy that could end it in a single stroke. The likely focus of that strategy would be to exploit Howe's capture of New York. This would entail making an attempt to divide the rebellious colonies in two, separating New England from those areas that still held large numbers of loyalists. Only by prying loyal Americans out of the grasp of the rebels could the war, for the British, be brought to a successful conclusion.

The Burgoyne Plan

Howe, for all of his skill at organizing and commanding armies, was a timid leader. He was by nature a cautious man, and he was known to harbor some sympathy for the American cause. Like many liberals in Britain, Howe felt that the colonial grievances had some merit to them. Rather than more fighting, the general would have preferred a negotiated settlement and reconciliation. He never lost hope in the possibility of reaching a peaceful settlement with his fellow British subjects. In short, Howe was not the best choice to execute a daring plan aimed at conquering New England, the hotbed of rebellion.

Burgoyne was a far better candidate. Burgoyne had arrived in America in June 1775 along with Howe and Clinton. Unlike his colleagues, however, Burgoyne favored an aggressive policy designed to end the rebellion quickly and

General Sir John Burgoyne developed and implemented a plan to crush the rebel forces.

hand in developing and implementing his plan for ending what he called an "unnatural Rebellion [headed by] the hardened enemies of Great Britain and America."[66]

Burgoyne envisioned a three-pronged assault that would cut off New England and deny Washington any hope of coming to its rescue. The main wings of the attacking force would move simultaneously down from Canada and up from New York City along a Hudson River axis. The third wing, actually a smaller army given the job of protecting Burgoyne's left flank, would head southward from Canada through the Mohawk Valley. It would eventually join the other two near Albany. Burgoyne would command the element moving south along the Hudson; Howe had the job of pushing upriver from New York City. The Mohawk Valley force would be led by Lieutenant colonel Barry St. Leger. Altogether, Burgoyne would have 8,300 men at his disposal, split roughly equally between British and German troops, including 650 Canadians and loyalist militiamen and 400 Iroquois Indians.

Howe and Philadelphia

Due to the unwise British command structure in America, Burgoyne could not compel Howe to follow his plan. He would have to trust that Howe would move up the Hudson on cue. Burgoyne

conclusively. It is not surprising, then, that it was Burgoyne who took the lead in crafting a plan to crush the rebel forces in 1777.

After the bloody engagement at Breed's Hill in 1775, London removed Gage from command in America. No one, however, replaced him as commander in chief. In fact, the highest-ranking official in North America was the governor of Canada, Sir Guy Carleton. Howe, Clinton, and Burgoyne, therefore, effectively shared authority for the use of the British forces. Burgoyne, as a result, had a free

had no way of knowing that Howe had others ideas. John Adams had once remarked that "Howe is a wild General,"[67] meaning that the general was an unpredictable man. And indeed he was. On this occasion in particular, Howe took everyone by surprise by ordering his troops to prepare for battle not up the Hudson but rather over 100 miles (161km) to the south in Pennsylvania. Without consulting Burgoyne, Howe had decided to attack Philadelphia, the seat of the Continental Congress. He would fulfill his obligation to Burgoyne by sending a token force upriver, but he intended to leave fully three thousand men sitting in New York City while taking the rest of his command, fifteen thousand soldiers, to the Chesapeake Bay by sea.

His force reached the outskirts of Philadelphia in early September and met Washington's army at Brandywine Creek. The American general had hurriedly moved his withered Continentals from their winter quarters in New Jersey as soon as he discovered that Howe's

Native America at War

During the Revolution, Native Americans took sides. By choice or through enticement, they threw in their lot with either the British or the colonists. Most allied themselves with the British. A long history of hostility and violence convinced most of them to fight against their traditional enemies, the colonists. For others, the decision was based on economics. Teaming up with the British would guarantee the continuation of lucrative trading arrangements. Whatever the reason, over thirteen thousand Indians fought alongside the king's men. These warriors were drawn from many tribes, most famously the Iroquois and Cherokee. Of the major Indian groups only the Oneida and Catawba allied themselves with the Americans. Put simply, the old battle lines between the colonists and Native Americans remained too bold to cross. The colonists despised the Indians, so the Indians turned to the British for partnership and long-term protection. The Indians remembered the proclamation line of 1763 and feared its erasure through American victory. The soon-to-be-independent Americans never forgave the Indians for what they considered to be treason. For decades after the war, the image lingered of Britons and Indians together attempting to crush the rebellion. The alliance only inflamed preexisting racial hatreds and served as an excuse for brutality.

ve was the American capital rather ob inking up with Burgoyne. On September 11 the two old adversaries did ttle once again, as they had in 1776. he outcome was the same. The Americans were defeated, and General Howe marched his men into Philadelphia just ahead of the now-panicked congress, which removed itself first to the town of Lancaster and then to York, Pennsylvania. Washington, determined not to give up such a prize as Philadelphia without a better fight, rallied his men for an attack on the northern edge of the British army. At Germantown, on October 4, 1777, Washington landed his blow, but the British won again. Dejected after losing two battles and a major American city, Washington took his troops west and settled them in at a place called Valley Forge. There he would endure a brutal winter that nearly cost him his entire army and his job as commander in chief.

Burgoyne Pushes South

Burgoyne had no intention of letting Howe ruin his effort to win the war. The general had long ago decided to drive on, no matter what the cost. "THIS ARMY MUST NOT RETREAT,"[68] he railed. With that, Burgoyne plunged southward. Almost from the start things began to go wrong. St. Leger's force stalled in the Mohawk Valley and was

This painting portrays the surrender of General Burgoyne at Saratoga.

The Continental Army and the Working Class

The call to arms in 1775 drew multitudes of citizen-soldiers to the rebel colors. They saw themselves as simple farmers whose virtue would win the day, battling in support of God-given liberty against tyranny. The brutal defeats of 1776 sent most of these early rebel recruits scurrying home. Although viewed today as heroes, many militiamen, in fact, proved to be just what Thomas Paine said they were—summer soldiers and sunshine patriots. They shrank from service when America needed them most. Beginning in 1777 a new kind of soldier fought for liberty against the most powerful army in the world. Lured into service by the promise of food, clothing, a twenty-dollar bonus, and a guarantee of 100 acres (40.5ha) of land after the war, thousands of working-class men joined the Continental army. They were white and black, immigrant and native born, but they shared in common a place at the bottom of the social ladder. They had nothing to offer or lose but their lives; they were men the rest of America considered expendable. "Once a long-term army became necessary, the public decided that it was the duty of only some men . . . to fill its ranks." Those "some men" were laborers, mechanics, and often slaves. Few monuments to their sacrifices were ever built.

Charles Royster, *A Revolutionary People at War: The Continental Army and American Character, 1775–1783.* New York: W.W. Norton, 1979, p. 129.

then turned back by a strong American contingent led by Arnold. The American force arrayed in front of him, moreover, was better equipped and better led than Burgoyne had anticipated. The efforts of Franklin to funnel French arms and ammunition to the Continental army had paid off; the American army in northern New York had plenty of both. More troubling for Burgoyne, his counterparts on the American side included not only the very able Arnold, but the equally formidable General Horatio Gates and Colonel Daniel Morgan. Without Howe's contribution, Burgoyne's army was at a distinct disadvantage in the coming fight.

Still, Burgoyne came. He slammed into the Americans on September 19 at Bemis Heights. Furious fighting ensued, in which the Americans matched their shooting skills against the British expertise with bayonets. An American officer remembered with awe the determination shown by the contesting forces. "Both armies," he wrote, "seemed determined to conquer or die. One continual blaze [of gunfire] without any intermission until dark, when by consent of both parties it ceased."[69] One of Burgoyne's officers recalled that the "crash of cannon

George Washington visits wounded soldiers at Valley Forge.

and musketry never ceased till darkness parted us."[70] By that time, both sides were exhausted and battered. Although Burgoyne technically won the engagement, his soldiers had been badly bloodied by the fierce American attacks.

Burgoyne tested his enemy again on October 7. This time the American troops, admirably led by Arnold, forced the British to retreat after a brutal fight. One of Britain's best generals was forced to admit that his men had been outfought and he had been "outgeneraled." On October 9 Burgoyne fell back to a position just outside Saratoga; three days later, Gates and Arnold surrounded him. Burgoyne and his entire force were left with no escape. The only option was to surrender. Negotiations began on October 16, 1777; the next day, Burgoyne gave his sword, fifty-eight hundred men, twenty-seven artillery pieces, and five thousand muskets to Gates. Upon meeting Gates, Burgoyne said calmly, "The fortunes of war, General, have made me your prisoner."[71] One of his generals, however, assessed the defeat in more emotional terms: "Poor General Burgoyne! Oh, fatal ambition!"[72] By order of the Confederation Congress, Burgoyne's officers and men were not allowed to return to England as Gates had promised in the surrender document, known as a convention. Only Burgoyne could go home. The rest of his force, known as the "Convention Army," was marched to

Virginia, there to sit out the war in relative peace and comfort.

A World War Begins

The consequences of Burgoyne's defeat at Saratoga became immediately apparent. Washington, trying to keep his demoralized and frostbitten army at Valley Forge from disintegrating, suddenly had one less enemy army to worry about. He could concentrate on resupplying his troops and training them to fight the British regulars on their own terms. He was aided in this task by invaluable advice and assistance from European officers who had signed on to the rebel cause. Chief among these volunteers were Casimir Pulaski, a Polish cavalryman, and Friedrich Wilhelm Steuben. Pulaski helped Washington create an effective cavalry corps to support his infantry, while Steuben was instrumental in training the Continental army in European battlefield tactics. Neither these men nor Washington himself could make the winter any warmer or food and medicine any more plentiful. Washington's army during that winter of 1777–1778 would suffer greatly. Yet the victory at Saratoga did promise to make Washington's job for the rest of 1778 and beyond a bit easier.

Washington was certainly heartened by another consequence of Gates's and Arnold's success: France finally decided to support fully and openly the revolutionary cause. Since the spring of 1776 arms and ammunition had been arriving in America through Rodrigue Hortalez and other smaller operations. These supplies had come almost exclusively from France, and they came in relative abundance. Indeed, Washington could thank covert French aid for keeping his army in the field against the British. Helpful as this was, however, America needed more. America needed the French army and navy. Only the addition of professional French soldiers and powerful French warships could turn the tide of war. To be sure, a few French volunteers were already holding Continental commands. The most famous was the young French nobleman Marie Joseph du Motier, the Marquis de Lafayette. Soon to distinguish himself during the southern campaign, Lafayette had arrived in America in 1777 and had fought alongside Washington at the battle of Brandywine. But such support was insufficient. The French had to come across the Atlantic in greater numbers as part of a formal alliance to make a real difference.

To date, though, Louis XVI had been reluctant to support the rebellion. He demanded clear evidence that the new republic could survive before he committed the power and prestige of France in support. He received the evidence he wanted with the victory at Saratoga. Gates and Arnold had proven that American armies could defeat their British counterparts in open-field battle. As a result, the king made the decision to form an alliance with America and throw the military might of France into the war, effectively turning the American Revolution into a world war. From India to the Caribbean, French and British forces would clash.

Benjamin Franklin attends a reception in Paris, France, in 1778. Franklin's efforts to funnel French arms and ammunition to the Continental army were successful, as the American army in northern New York had plenty of both.

Negotiations began between the government of Vergennes and the American team led by Franklin, now the senior member of the Franklin-Adams-Lee committee that had been in France for almost two years. Deane had since returned to America. After long talks the American and French representatives settled on the precise wording of a Treaty of Amity and Commerce, which was signed by both parties on February 6, 1778. According to the treaty's provisions, it pledged France and America to a "defensive alliance [that] is to maintain effectually the liberty, sovereignty, and independence of the said United States, as well in matters of government as of commerce."[73] France and America would trade with one another and fight side by side "until the moment of the cessation of the present war between the United States and England."[74] Soon, French soldiers were boarding ships, preparing to sail for war against the British in America once again.

The Southern Strategy

The disaster at Saratoga and news of the French-American treaty forced parliament to take action. Blamed for everything that had happened in 1777, Howe was relieved of his command and replaced by Clinton. If Clinton hoped to inherit a promising situation, he was soon disappointed. The news throughout the first half of 1778 was relentlessly bad for the British. France and Britain were now at war around the world, and reports had arrived that a French ship carrying thousands of veteran soldiers was making its way toward New England. An American army west of the Mississippi had crushed Britain's Indian allies. Howe's occupying force in Philadelphia had been ordered to withdraw to New York, only to be stru[ck] in New Jersey by a newly co[nfident] Washington, who had rolled out of Valley Forge in June. The loss of Burgoyne's army had reduced British troop strength by almost half, and the initiative in the war had seemed to pass to the Americans and their new French allies.

Clinton's troubles were multiplied by a parliament that had grown weary of war. More members than ever wanted to bring the fighting to a close, even if it meant negotiating with rebels. Arriving in New York in October, a commission headed by William Eden, the earl

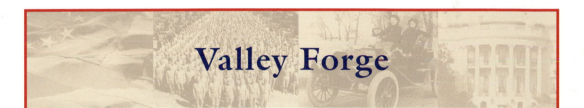

Valley Forge

In the fall of 1777 George Washington took his battered army into winter quarters at Valley Forge, Pennsylvania. Twenty miles (32.2km) away, his opponent, General Howe, rested comfortably in Philadelphia. Howe actually looked forward to a lull in the fighting; Washington prayed simply to endure it. The winter of 1777–1778 was a harsh one. Men left camp in a steady stream, unable to cope with the hardships of winter. Soldiers lived in tiny huts in groups of twelve. Clothing became scarce, leading frequently to debilitating frostbite. Sickness and hunger soon followed. When flour ran short, men used sawdust to make biscuits called "fire cakes." Washington did the best he could to withstand the weather and prevent the desertion of his troops. He struggled to get supplies and occupied his men with training exercises and drills led by the Baron von Steuben. All the while, he had to defend himself against the efforts of a small group of officers to have him relieved of command. Known to history as the "Conway Cabal," after its leader Thomas Conway, the group lobbied to have Washington replaced by General Horatio Gates. They failed, and Washington held his post. His army survived the winter and went on to victory.

of Carlisle, tried to get the congress to enter into peace talks. Emboldened by the British failures and defeats, the Americans were in no mood to talk, and the Carlisle Commission departed without making any progress. Parliament also let Clinton know that further spending on the war effort would be limited, and new troop assignments would not be made. Clinton, in essence, was on his own to do the best he could with the resources at his disposal. Now, as it was with Washington in 1776, the war was Clinton's to win or lose. He aimed to win it.

Doing this meant moving south. Clinton and his new subordinate, Cornwallis, felt certain that a British army operating in the southern colonies would be able to supply itself with troops and materiel drawn directly from the land. Both generals believed that the majority of people in the South were loyal to the crown and would readily offer support and fighting forces to any British commander. As Germain put it, "Large numbers of the inhabitants [of the South] would flock to the King's standard and . . . His Majesty's Government would be restored."[75] True, an attempt to take Charleston, South Car-

John Paul Jones

John Paul Jones was Revolutionary America's only naval commander of note, and the battles he fought were the only significant engagements involving the American navy. Born John Paul in Scotland in 1747, he went to sea at the age of twelve. As a boy he learned everything he could about the ships of the day. Jones ran into trouble, however, as a young man. He was accused of murder and forced to flee to America, adding the name "Jones" along the way to hide his identity. After joining the navy he compiled an impressive record. Jones captured sixteen British ships before being dispatched to European waters. There he raided the English coast and attacked merchant shipping. In September 1779 he was finally cornered by the royal navy off Flamborough Head. Jones, commanding the *Bonhomme Richard*, faced off against a number of British vessels, the most dangerous being the *Serapis*. What followed was a classic eighteenth-century sea battle. Locked together by grappling hooks, the *Bonhomme Richard* and *Serapis* pounded away at one another. After a ferocious fight, the *Serapis* surrendered. Jones's victory was celebrated throughout America and is counted as the American navy's first triumph. John Paul Jones died quietly in France in 1792.

olina, in 1776 had failed miserably, but Clinton attributed that to lack of will and competence on Howe's part. Clinton was sure that he would succeed where his predecessor had not. A powerful force, under Cornwallis's command, would be landed in the Carolinas. From there the regulars would move inland, where they would be welcomed as liberators by the loyal people yearning to escape from "Congress' tyranny."[76] Along the way, Cornwallis's army would destroy the rebels and establish a solid base of operations for the conquest of the northern colonies, including New England.

A Very Good Start

In November 1778 Clinton sent a small invasion force of three thousand five hundred and fifty men south from New York with orders to capture the town of Savannah, Georgia. The soldiers would be assisted by two thousand British troops marching north from Florida. The advance north was more rapid than even Clinton had expected. The units from New York linked up easily with their comrades. Savannah was quickly cleared of rebels, and British general in charge could report triumphantly on December 29 that "the capital of Georgia . . . fell into our possession before it was dark."[77] One of his American opponents, commenting on the minimal British casualties, noted that "never was a victory of such magnitude so completely gained with so little loss."[78] Augusta, Georgia, fell to the British a month later. By early February 1779, Georgia was under British control, and Clinton could now plan his masterstroke, an invasion of the Carolinas.

The next spring and summer were given over to preparations for the shift of British forces southward. Clinton planned to hold New York City with a force sufficient to keep Washington occupied, while sending five thousand men and fourteen warships to attack and "possibly get possession of Charlestown."[79] If his scheme worked, the war might end as early as the middle of 1780. As he departed New York City on December 29, 1779, Clinton had no idea that a new war and not just a new campaign was about to begin.

Chapter Six

The Road to Yorktown, 1780–1781

Clinton's plan to conquer the South was nothing if not ambitious. He knew that time was running short; the king, parliament, and the British public were losing patience with the army in America. What the general needed most was a quick and decisive victory won without great expense of money or lives, a victory that would end the conflict with the American rebels. Clinton certainly never intended to initiate what became essentially a new and different kind of war. Yet that is precisely what happened. The southern campaign would be fought on two fronts. On the one hand, set-piece battles were planned in which the British would meet their American and French opponents on the traditional field of battle, as had happened in the North between 1775 and 1777. On the other hand, Clinton and his campaign commander Cornwallis had to put the loyalist troops at their disposal to good use. The loyalists knew well the country and their rebel antagonists. They would play a big role in the upcoming contest. The dual character of the combat strategy and the prospect of Americans killing Americans meant that the southern war would be very different from its northern counterpart. The difference extended to the outcome, in this case American success that would lead to independence.

Charleston

Clinton had chosen Charleston, South Carolina, as the point of entry for his invasion force. This was not the first time a British task force had targeted Charleston. In 1776 an amphibious assault was turned back in the face of fierce American resistance. Clinton had studied that earlier effort and decided to alter one crucial detail in the repeat performance. Rather than attacking from the sea, the general planned to land his troops outside the city and march to the landward side. He accomplished this soon after putting ashore in April 1780. Swinging his soldiers around to the less well-defended side, Clinton essentially cut the city off. Once in position, British engineers began constructing a series of trenches that would protect the rest of the force as it pushed to within artillery range of Charleston. Meanwhile, the British fleet closed off the shipping routes into the city. Clinton now intended to pound Charleston into submission.

Inside the beleaguered port, the American commander General Benjamin Lincoln was confident that he could hold out. His defenses were well prepared, and he had an escape route. Thirty miles (48km) north of the city, a small mounted force of Continentals held an important road open for Lincoln and the Charleston defenders should they need to use it to escape. As long as the cavalry was in place, Lincoln could sit and wait.

Clinton had other ideas. After learning of the existence of the covering force, he dispatched Colonel Sir Banastre Tarleton and his Green Dragoons, otherwise known as the American Legion, to destroy it. Tarleton, son of a wealthy merchant, was a daring officer known for his ferocity, intelligence, and fighting skills. His unit consisted of British cavalry and loyalist horsemen who despised the rebellion and wanted nothing more than to kill men they considered to be criminals and traitors. On April 13 Tarleton swooped

down on the Americans and crushed them. Tarleton recorded how American "officers and men who attempted to defend themselves were killed,"[80] often with bayonets. Others fled to the surrounding swamps where they were hunted down. The luckiest of the Americans hid in the woods until nightfall and then slipped away.

When news of the defeat reached Lincoln, he immediately knew that he could no longer resist Clinton's siege. The British cannons were pouring shells into Charleston, and every route out of the

General Sir Henry Clinton came up with a plan to invade the southern colonies.

Colonel Sir Banastre Tarleton led the Green Dragoons.

city had been severed by either British troops or ships. The American general William Moultrie described the bombardment that took place on May 7: "The fire was incessant almost the whole night, cannon balls whizzing and shells hissing continually among us, ammunition chests and temporary magazines blowing up, great guns exploding, and wounded men groaning along the lines. It was a dreadful night! It was our last great effort, but it availed us nothing."[81] Five days later, Lincoln, thirty-six hun-

dred Continentals, and eighteen hundred rebel militiamen surrendered to Clinton. The Carolinas lay open to the British.

Camden

Clinton was now free to move inland and begin the campaign he had longed for. Events, however, prevented him from leading the upcoming fight himself. The general's intelligence officers reported that a French fleet was headed toward New York, forcing him to return to his base in the north. Clinton put four thousand men aboard ship and sailed away from Charleston, leaving Cornwallis and Tarleton to conduct operations as they saw fit. Here, the war turned in a bloody new direction. The British commanders went their own ways. Cornwallis began preparing to move on the American main force near Camden; Tarleton made it his mission to hunt down rebel militias and slaughter them.

While Cornwallis organized his army, Tarleton and his Green Dragoons rode to Waxhaw, near the border with North Carolina. There he overwhelmed a force of Virginia militia, which promptly surrendered. Yet, instead of collecting the men together as prisoners of war, Tarleton ordered his horsemen to cut the Americans down. The dragoons showed no mercy. The defenseless men were bayoneted. The British then went over the bodies "plunging their bayonets into everyone that exhibited any signs of life."[82] The massacre at Waxhaw earned Tarleton the nickname "Bloody Ban," and it would not be the last time that men trying to surrender would suffer such a fate. Tarleton's brutality unleashed forces of disorder and mayhem that would prove difficult for both sides to restrain.

While Tarleton was busy murdering prisoners, Cornwallis marched against the American army at Camden. His opponents actually comprised something less than an army. When Gates, the hero of Saratoga, took command of the Continentals who would oppose the British in South Carolina, they numbered only fourteen hundred weary men. Throughout the summer of 1780, Gates worked to get his

This is a depiction of the aftermath of the Waxhaw Massacre.

troops into fighting condition. In early August Gates's ranks were swelled by the arrival of twenty-one hundred North Carolina militiamen and a contingent of militia from Virginia. By the middle of the month the American commander felt confident that he could take on and defeat Cornwallis's advancing redcoats.

Gates's men were determined to fight, but their general had planned the upcoming battle poorly. When Gates met Cornwallis, he placed his militia rather than his better-trained Continentals opposite hardened regulars. In the fight that followed, the British smashed through the militia and threatened to encircle the entire American army. At the mere sight of Cornwallis's men, the North Carolinians and Virginians panicked and ran. The Continentals held on a little longer, but soon they too were in full retreat. No American on the field that day fled as quickly as Gates himself. He mounted the fastest horse he could find and rode away from his command. By nightfall Gates had covered sixty miles (96.6km) in headlong flight. General Washington's young aide, Alexander Hamilton, asked bitterly, "Was there ever an instance of a general running away . . . from his whole army?"[83] Gates's performance at Camden was an embarrassment, and his defeat opened the way for Cornwallis to advance through the Carolinas and perhaps into Virginia. Desperate times had returned for the rebellion.

A Hero's Treason

The sting of Camden was aggravated by events far to the north, in New York.

Arnold had always been a proud man, but his success at Saratoga left him with a grossly inflated sense of achievement. Arnold felt that he deserved a much greater share of the prestige and power that went to men like Washington. He began to imagine that the congress held a grudge against him and blamed that for his failure to rise in rank. Arnold, moreover, considered his assignments after Saratoga to be calculated insults, none more so than his appointment as commander of the fort at West Point.

Arnold viewed the assignment as beneath him, and his wife encouraged his sense of injury. Peggy Shippen Arnold was a beautiful young girl whom Arnold had met in Philadelphia after the British evacuated the city. She had always harbored secret loyalist sympathies and now began to prod her husband to avenge his honor. Mrs. Arnold had already introduced her husband to a dashing British officer, Major John André, who made it clear to the American general that aiding the crown would be the best way to get back at Washington and the congress. The command at West Point provided Arnold with an opportunity to take André up on his offer.

By mid-September 1780 Arnold had given André the plans to the fort and had agreed to open its defenses to a British attack that very month. A British seizure of West Point would have erased any hope Washington had of eventually recapturing New York City. This fact made Arnold's treason all the more dangerous.

Francis Marion at the Movies

Mel Gibson's movie *The Patriot* (2000) offered a fictionalized account of irregular warfare in the South during the Revolution. More specifically, the film traced broadly the life of the South Carolina rebel guerilla leader Francis Marion. Nicknamed "the Swamp Fox," he was the model for Gibson's character, Benjamin Martin. In the film, Martin is a reluctant rebel, driven to violence by the murder of his young son. The killer, Colonel Tavington (patterned after Banastre Tarleton), thus becomes Martin's nemesis. The movie then follows the main character as he battles the British toward a final showdown with Tavington and ultimate victory for the rebel cause. Although the Hollywood incarnation of Francis Marion fought for liberty, the real-life guerilla and his men often had less heroic goals. Looting, stealing loyalist land, and settling personal scores many times proved more important to them than independence. Men like Marion, in fact, rarely acted nobly and matched the brutality of their opponents. American guerillas killed prisoners, burned homes, and terrorized innocent people. Yet in one important respect, the film captured reality. The activities of rebel bands, like the one led by Marion, hindered British operations and helped to force decisive battles such as Cowpens, Guilford Courthouse, and Yorktown.

The plot was foiled on September 25. After a secret meeting with André, Arnold prepared for an inspection by none other than George Washington. When the commander in chief arrived, however, Arnold was nowhere to be found. His soldiers reported that he had left in a hurry before Washington got there, taking only a few personal items and saying a quick goodbye to his wife and child. The general inspected West Point as planned and was disturbed to find it in disrepair and its defenses weak. This puzzled Washington. Arnold had always been such a precise man; Washington could not figure out why the fort was in such a sorry state.

His answer came in a set of papers brought to him by his aide, Hamilton. André had been captured by an American patrol after leaving West Point. The plans to the fort and details of Arnold's treachery were discovered inside one of his boots. Arnold, having heard of the arrest before Washington showed up, was safely aboard a British warship when his commander learned of his plot to betray America. "My God!" Washington exclaimed, "Arnold has gone over to the British. Whom can we trust now?"[84]

In an act of treason, Benedict Arnold instructs John André to hide the plans to the fort at West Point in his boot.

His scheme uncovered, Arnold had no choice but to do the best he could as a newly loyal British subject: He took a command in the British army and prepared to leave for Virginia wearing a red coat. His wife and son were heartbroken by his departure but were well treated by the Americans, on Washington's order. André was not so lucky. He had been captured in civilian clothes, which, by the laws of war, made him a spy. He was hanged after putting the rope around his own neck and telling his executioners, "Only bear witness that I died a brave man."[85]

Greene and Morgan: A New Beginning

As André was being executed, the southern war began in earnest. Tarleton had always operated semi-independently from Cornwallis. Both officers agreed that while Cornwallis tackled the Continental forces, Tarleton would throw his dragoons into the struggle against the rebel militias. His ruthlessness and that of his loyalist troops were seen as the only antidote to the scourge of mobile irregular warfare that plagued the southern campaign. Cornwallis's supply lines and rear areas were never safe from the rebel bands that roamed the countryside. Rebel fighters conducted hit-and-run attacks wherever and whenever they could, and their efforts were paying off. Cornwallis was compelled to slow his march through the backcountry as he dealt with the irritating rebel raids. Tarleton was assigned to suppress the rebel marauders any way he could.

The first step, Tarleton decided, was to deal with the better-organized militia forces first, leaving the loosely structured guerilla units for later. This job he gave to Major Patrick Ferguson, a solid officer who commanded 150 regulars and 900 loyalists. Ferguson aggressively sought battle with the rebels and gained it in October 1780 at King's Mountain in South Carolina. Fighting a pitched battle with rebel militiamen, Ferguson's troops were defeated. In retaliation for Tarleton's brutality, the victorious American rebels slaughtered any American loyalists taken prisoner. King's Mountain was yet another example of how

The feverish Battle of King's Mountain is shown here.

closely the southern war resembled a civil war.

Despite its bloody finale, the battle of King's Mountain energized the American forces in the Carolinas. Guerilla attacks against British troops increased dramatically. Irregular units commanded by men such as Francis Marion, "the Swamp Fox," and Thomas Sumter, "the Carolina Gamecock," took a steady toll on Cornwallis's expedition and became ever bolder. Rebel militias attacked their loyalist counterparts relentlessly. So many Americans were killing each other that one loyalist reported that South Car-olina "resembled a piece of patchwork,"[86] with neighbor fighting neighbor.

American successes in late 1780 also encouraged the aggressiveness of Gates's replacements in the Carolinas, General Nathanael Greene and his able assistant Morgan. Greene and Morgan had been assigned the difficult task of keeping Cornwallis from extending his reach northward into North Carolina and Virginia. Given the right circumstances and a sound plan, the two Americans were certain that they could do just that. The first step would be to force Tarleton to suspend his irregular operations and

Patrick Ferguson's Rifle

Major Patrick Ferguson gained lasting fame for his decision not to shoot George Washington at Brandywine Creek. He chose to let the American general live because "it was not pleasant to fire at the back of an unoffending individual . . . so I let him alone." Ferguson is also remembered for his role in the losing British effort at King's Mountain in 1780, a battle in which he lost his life. He is less well known as the inventor of the "Ferguson rifle," an early experiment in breech-loading firearms. Eighteenth-century rifled muskets were very accurate but slow to load and difficult to maintain. The reason lay in the fact that they had to be loaded from the front, the muzzle end. The obvious remedy was to make a gun that loaded from the rear, the breech end. Ferguson was one of many inventors who set out to do that. He ended up being more successful than most and produced a fine weapon that combined accuracy and ease of care with rapidity of fire. The British army, oddly enough, showed little interest in Ferguson's rifle; it was never seriously considered for adoption as a standard firearm. Breech-loading guns were neither mass-produced nor widely used until the middle of the nineteenth century.

rejoin Cornwallis's main army. Then the British regulars and Tarleton's dragoons could be defeated at once, leaving the Carolinas in the hands of the Continental army and its militia auxiliaries. Boldness and daring were called for, and Greene and Morgan had plenty of both.

Cowpens and Guilford Courthouse

Violating a central rule of war, Greene and Morgan divided their forces during the winter of 1780–1781 and went looking for their enemies. Greene, it was planned, would handle Cornwallis while Morgan took care of diverting the attention of Tarleton's mobile force. Neither Greene nor Morgan ever imagined that Tarleton's legion would be brought to battle and nearly annihilated. But that is exactly what happened. On January 17, 1781, Morgan met Tarleton near the border with North Carolina.

The place was called Cowpens, and it was perfectly suited for the type of combat Morgan preferred. Backed up against the water, his less-than-reliable militia would be forced to fight hard, but that did not really matter to Morgan. He expected the militia line to break when Tarleton's eleven hundred British regulars and loyalists struck it. That is why he placed his trustworthy Continentals in a camouflaged position behind the militia. Once in position, Morgan waited for the British to assemble and prepared for Tarleton's charge. When it came, Morgan broke it and sent Tarleton's men reeling backward. By noon the battle was over. One hundred British

soldiers had been killed and eight hundred taken prisoner. With a mere forty cavalrymen, Tarleton limped back to Cornwallis to report on his defeat.

Cornwallis was now more determined than ever to smash Greene and Morgan. He immediately set out after the Americans, who had brought their commands back together, and caught them on March 15, 1781, at Guilford Courthouse in North Carolina. Yet Cornwallis caught hold of more than he could handle. He had with him twenty-two hundred troops compared to nearly forty-five hundred Americans; for once, Greene and Morgan had the advantage. They intended to use it. Morgan urged Greene to replay the battle of Cowpens. "Put the riflemen on the flanks," he advised, "Put the militia in the centre, with some picked troops in their rear with orders to shoot down the first man that runs."[87] Greene took the advice and arranged his defenses in three separate lines with militia to the front and Continentals in the rear.

Eager for battle, Cornwallis launched his force directly at the Americans. Through a hail of musket balls, the British rushed forward. When the first line finally broke, the redcoats pushed on toward the second, which collapsed. At the third line, however, the Americans stood their ground, trading a vicious fire with their British opponents. Cornwallis himself had a horse shot out from under him but continued to lead his troops forward. Pouring artillery fire into the American line, the British fought furiously. Finally, Greene, fearing his army might collapse, ordered a general retreat.

The Battle of Cowpens, January 17, 1781, was a swift victory for the Americans.

Cornwallis had won, but his men were too exhausted to pursue their foes. On April 25 Cornwallis left a small army behind to harass the Americans and took the bulk of his ravaged army into Virginia. There he planned to rest and resupply his troops, then join up with Arnold, newly commissioned a brigadier general, in a quest to conquer Virginia and clear the Carolinas of rebels. Cornwallis himself wanted to remain in the interior of Virginia, but Clinton had other considerations. He needed Cornwallis's army to be close to the sea, just in case New York came under attack. Clinton suggested that Cornwallis choose a base of operations closer to navigable rivers and the Chesapeake Bay. The spot that best fit that description was the peninsula between the York and James rivers, in particular the port of Yorktown.

The World Turns Upside Down in Virginia

By the end of July 1781, Cornwallis had finished gathering his troops at Yorktown and had completed a series of impressive fortifications around it. Washington, at this time, had been conducting minor operations around New York while waiting for a French fleet to arrive that would bring thousands of French soldiers to his command. The previous May he and the French general Jean-Baptiste-Donatien de Vimeur, Comte de Rochambeau, had decided to attack Clinton as soon as the reinforcements arrived. When the two learned of Cornwallis's movement, however, they sent a message to the admiral in command, François-Joseph-Paul Comte de Grasse, to turn his ships toward the Chesapeake Bay and meet them there. The French-American army then slipped quietly away from its station around New York City and marched toward Yorktown.

Washington left two thousand five hundred men along the Hudson River to hide his movement and took 5,000 French and 2,000 American soldiers south with him. By early September, with his army nearing Virginia, Washington learned that part of Cornwallis's command had been shipped back to New York to reinforce Clinton. The general increased the pace of his march. Meanwhile, the French fleet had arrived and had landed 3,000 French soldiers near Yorktown; they immediately linked up with a small contingent of Americans, led by Lafayette, that had been monitoring Cornwallis. Sensing trouble, Clinton ordered a fleet southward to rescue Cornwallis, but it arrived too late. On September 6 the French navy

General Charles O'Hara surrenders for Cornwallis at Yorktown on October 19, 1781.

turned the British ships back. Cornwallis was on his own. Washington and Rochambeau arrived on September 28 and laid siege to Yorktown with a mighty army of more than 16,000 men.

For over a month the French and American artillery pounded Cornwallis's positions. Fierce counterattacks by the British failed to break through the allied lines on land, and no relief fleet could break in from the sea. The British were trapped. As the days passed, conditions inside Yorktown worsened. Food supplies ran low; the wounded suffered without medicine or proper care. Worst of all, the incoming artillery fire was unrelenting. A doctor accompanying Washington wrote that "a tremendous and incessant firing from the American and French batteries is kept up, and the enemy return the fire, but with little effect."[88] On the other side of the trenches, the British complained that they "could find no refuge in or out of the town. The people fled to the waterside and hid in hastily contrived shelters on the banks, but many of them were killed by bursting bombs."[89]

Cornwallis had no choice. His lines were crumbling, and soon the French

The French Navy at Yorktown

Credit for helping America win its independence usually goes to the French army and its celebrated officers, the Comte de Rochambeau and the Marquis de Lafayette. The French navy, however, is perhaps more worthy of that honor. Ships under the command of men such as Charles Comte d'Estaing, Louis Comte d'Barre, and François-Joseph-Paul Comte de Grasse played a crucial role in the war, in particular the battle of Yorktown. When Grasse's fleet appeared in the Chesapeake Bay that January 1781, it signaled the end of Cornwallis's southern campaign. Grasse sealed off Cornwallis's only escape route and completed the encirclement of the British begun by Washington and Rochambeau. The French warships then turned back a relief force commanded by the British admiral Sir Thomas Graves, winning arguably the most important naval battle of the war. The size and obvious power of Grasse's fleet persuaded General Clinton that any further effort to rescue Cornwallis would be a waste of energy and resources. Without hope from the sea, Cornwallis was compelled to surrender. As powerful as it was, the combined French-American army could not have won at Yorktown without the French navy.

and Americans would punch their way in. On October 17 he dispatched an officer carrying a white flag to speak with Washington about terms of surrender. As Cornwallis later told Clinton, he saw it as "wanton and inhuman . . . to sacrifice the lives of [his] gallant soldiers . . . by exposing them to an assault which, from the numbers and precautions of the enemy, could not fail to succeed."[90] Washington received the British officer and informed him that his commander could sign surrender papers in the morning. The British flags were to be rolled up, and the army's weapons would be stacked in front of the French-American lines.

The British marched out of Yorktown on October 19, 1781. Cornwallis was not with them. He claimed to be too sick to attend the ceremonies and left it to one of his aides to surrender the army. General Charles O'Hara at first offered his sword to Rochambeau. It was refused; the French general pointed to Washington. When O'Hara approached Washington and once again held out the blade, the general said courteously, "Never from such a good hand,"[91] and motioned toward Lincoln, who accepted it. As the redcoats sadly filed forward and stacked their arms, an American drummer and fifers played a tune everyone recognized. The words came into all the heads present at Yorktown:

> If ponies rode men and if grass ate
> cows,
> And cats should be chased into
> holes by the mouse . . .
> If summer were spring and the other
> way round,
> Then all the world would be upside
> down.

When Clinton was informed of Cornwallis's surrender, he knew that the war was lost.

Novus Ordo Seclorum: A New Order of the Ages, 1781–1789

After Yorktown, the war dragged on for another two years. The fighting, however, was located almost entirely outside of North America. Clinton, alone with his army in New York, was able to do little besides launch occasional raids here and there against isolated coastal towns. Washington, having moved north again after Cornwallis's surrender, had the unfortunate Clinton bottled up. Headquartered at Newburgh, the Continental army had the British surrounded. Clinton's was a waiting game now, waiting for peace and a formal end to the war.

The International War

Relative calm might have returned to mainland America, but overseas and in the Caribbean it was a different matter altogether. There the war heated up. Spain had been a nominal ally of the United States since 1779. In truth, Spain was technically an ally only of France,

and through France it became a partner of the United States. Regardless of the connection, the military effect was the same: Spanish participation in the fighting was bad news for Britain. Spain's entry into the conflict, in fact, according to the historian John Shy, "set off a new wave of panic in London and New York."[92] Spanish help, especially at sea, increased the already heavy pressure on Britain and drew critical British resources away from the main war effort. Together, the French and Spanish gave Britain no rest from its troubles.

No sooner had the land war ended in America than the one at sea intensified. Major naval operations took place around the world. Fierce sea battles raged off the coast of South Africa, in the West Indies, and in the waters of the Indian Ocean. In September 1782 a combined French-Spanish fleet attacked the British fortress at Gibraltar in the Mediterranean. For months the joint task force pummeled

Gibraltar, but the garrison held out. The British, in this case at least, could claim victory. Yet the international war at sea proved costly. As historian Geoffrey Perret has noted, Spain's participation "distracted the British on a worldwide scale. . . . At some point something would have to give. The British held on to Gibraltar—and lost America."[93]

Peace and Beyond

While fleets of tall ships wrestled with one another at sea, politicians on land began the peace process. Humiliated by the utter defeat of the British armies in America, North's government in London crumbled. George III replaced him with William Petty Fitzmaurice, the earl of Shelburne. Shelburne had always secretly sympathized with the Americans. Now he hoped to arrange a peace that might recognize American independence while maintaining the old colonial trading relationship. Shelburne felt that even if the Americans went their own way, Britain could still dominate the new nation's markets. He wanted, in short, to end the war in a way that benefited both parties.

By November 1782 British and American negotiators meeting in Paris had reached an agreement. According to the terms of the 1778 alliance, neither the Americans nor the French could make a separate peace with Britain. The first accord, then, was called a preliminary agreement rather than a treaty. Yet it functioned the same way. Faced with the reality of an obvious deal between America and Britain, and hoping to keep the two English-speaking countries as far apart as possible, the French went along with the deal.

In the spirit of Shelburne, the terms of the peace were very generous. To begin with, all British troops would leave America, beginning with those in New York now under the command of Carleton. Great Britain next agreed to recognize the independence of the United States and give it vast tracts of land. The new nation's borders would stretch from the Atlantic coast to the Mississippi River

The Treaty of Paris was signed on September 3, 1783, thus ending the American Revolution.

and from Canada to Florida. In return the United States promised to pay off prewar debts left over from the colonial period and to protect the rights of former loyalists. The British kept control of Canada, thus cheating France out the prize it went to war for in the first place. Nevertheless, France consented to this and the rest of the treaty's provisions. The document, known simply as the Treaty of Paris, was signed on September 3, 1783. The American Revolution was over. The colonies, after eight long years of war, were officially the free and independent United States of America.

From Confederation to Constitution

The next four years were filled with turmoil. Another change in government in London brought to power an anti-American faction. Soon policies were put into place that discriminated against the young American republic. Britain closed the West Indies to almost all American trade, refused to leave its forts on American soil near the Great Lakes, and began supplying hostile Indian tribes with guns. Spain, freed from any obligation to the United States by the coming of peace, closed the Mississippi River to American traffic in 1785. The American economy slowed and threatened to collapse altogether.

Faced with such grave problems in foreign relations, the Confederation Congress, the American government since 1781, sat paralyzed. It had taken four years for the various states to ratify the Articles of Confederation written in 1777. The reason for the delay was simple:

Revolutionary Americans did not trust central authority. Most people felt that a small, weak national government would be the best guarantee of continued liberty. Consequently they gave very little power to the Confederation Congress when it was finally established. The congress could raise neither taxes nor armies and had almost no ability to regulate trade. Perhaps worst of all, it could not force the individual states to do what was needed for the common good. Each state seemed to go its own way.

Without money, troops, or the ability to make binding decisions for the states, the congress had little influence in foreign relations; everyone doubted its ability to protect the nation from foreign enemies or those closer to home. American debt was soaring. Working people and farmers were going broke. Unrest became common in the cities and in the countryside. In Massachusetts, a Revolutionary War veteran named Daniel Shays led a farm uprising that ended only when militiamen were called in to suppress it.

Even George Washington was shocked by the situation. Writing to his wartime artillery chief, Henry Knox, Washington complained that the troubles betrayed the ideals of the Revolution itself. "I feel, my dear General Knox," Washington said, "infinitely more than I can express to you, for the disorders which have arisen in these States. Good God!"[94] He also worried openly that if the British sensed American weakness in incidents like Shays's Rebellion, it might just attack. "That Great Britain will be an unconcerned spectator of the present insurrections, if they continue, is not to be expected . . . she is at this moment sowing the seeds of jealousy and discontent among the various tribes of Indians on our frontiers."[95]

Something had to be done, or the history of the United States might just end in the 1780s. That something was a new constitution to replace the crumbling Articles of Confederation. Engineered by James Madison and Hamilton, a call went out for a convention of the states to meet in Philadelphia in May 1787. By September the delegates had reorganized the American government. The new United States Congress was granted more authority to combat the economic and foreign policy problems facing the country. The federal system created by the Constitution made the national government stronger than the states, gave it the power to tax, and allowed it to declare and wage war. The Constitution also provided for a chief executive, a president, to ensure that the will of Congress was enforced. To Americans at the time, especially those sitting in Philadelphia, it seemed obvious who the first president of the United States would be.

The Federalist Papers

The Constitution, after months of work, was finished in September 1787. The next step was ratification by the individual states through popular conventions. The people of the states, rather than the state governments, would approve or disapprove of the new document. So if they hoped to secure passage, the Constitution's supporters would have to appeal directly to the American people. It would not be an easy job. Most Americans were reluctant to give more power to a distant central government controlled by the established political elite. The Revolution, many argued, had promised that power would be kept local and in the hands of the common folk. Now the writers of the Constitution wanted to change all that. People were suspicious. In order to address those suspicions, James Madison, Alexander Hamilton, and John Jay used the widespread and widely read newspapers of the day to distribute a series of short essays known as the *Federalist Papers*. The essays covered a broad range of topics, including presidential authority, taxation and representation, and the division of power between the national and state governments. The newspaper plan worked; Americans were persuaded to support the Constitution. The only addition was a Bill of Rights to guarantee individual liberty.

The electoral college voted unanimously in 1788 for George Washington. He was inaugurated in April 1789.

A New Future

The decades ahead would see their share of danger and difficulty. Many times it looked like the United States would fail. Each time, however, it survived. "Our constitution is in actual operation," Benjamin Franklin famously said, "everything appears to promise that it will last; but nothing is certain in this world but death and taxes." Nothing is or was certain, but from the ruins of an empire a new republic rose up. The American Revolution produced notions of liberty, justice, and equality that changed the way people think about society and politics. In this sense, it did indeed create a genuine and enduring "new order of the ages."

Notes

Introduction: A Troubled Family

1. Jack P. Greene, ed., *Settlements to Society, 1607–1763: A Documentary History of Colonial America*. New York: W.W. Norton, 1975, p. 8.
2. John J. McCusker and Russell R. Menard, *The Economy of British America, 1607–1789*. Chapel Hill: University of North Carolina Press, 1985, p. 39.
3. Edmund Morgan, *Inventing the People: The Rise of Popular Sovereignty in England and America*. New York: W.W. Norton, 1988, p. 133.
4. Quoted in John Ferling, *Struggle for a Continent: The Wars of Early America*. Arlington Heights, IL: Harlan Davidson, 1993, p. 205.
5. Quoted in Ferling, *Struggle for a Continent*, p. 206.

Chapter One: Sugar and Stamps, 1763–1766

6. Henry Steele Commager, ed., *Documents of American History*. New York: Appleton-Century-Crofts, 1958, p. 47.
7. Quoted in Commager, *Documents of American History*, p. 49.
8. Quoted in Commager, *Documents of American History*, p. 50.
9. Quoted in A.J. Langguth, *Patriots: The Men Who Started the American Revolution*. New York: Simon & Schuster, 1988, p. 49.
10. Quoted in Commager, *Documents of American History*, p. 56.
11. Quoted in Commager, *Documents of American History*, p. 58.
12. Bernard Bailyn, *The Ordeal of Thomas Hutchinson*. Cambridge, MA: Belknap Press of the Harvard University Press, 1974, p. 37.
13. Quoted in Bailyn, *Ordeal of Thomas Hutchinson*, p. 36.
14. Quoted in Bailyn, *Ordeal of Thomas Hutchinson*, p. 110.
15. Quoted in Commager, *Documents of American History*, p. 61.

Chapter Two: From Townsend to Tea, 1767–1773

16. Quoted in Commager, *Documents of American History*, p. 63.
17. Quoted in Robert Harvey, *"A Few Bloody Noses": The Realities and Myths of the American Revolution*. New York: Overlook, 2001, p. 79.
18. Quoted in Commager, *Documents of American History*, p. 66.
19. Quoted in Robert Middlekauff, *The Glorious Cause: The American Revolution, 1763–1789*. New York: Oxford University Press, 1982, p. 169.

20. Quoted in Langguth, *Patriots*, p. 101.

21. Quoted in Bailyn, *Ordeal of Thomas Hutchinson*, p. 123

22. Benson Bobrick, *Angel in the Whirlwind: The Triumph of the American Revolution.* New York: Simon & Schuster, 1997, pp. 82-83

23. Quoted in Bobrick, *Angel in the Whirlwind*, p. 83

24. Quoted in Harvey, *A Few Bloody Noses*, p. 101.

25. Quoted in Langguth, *Patriots*, p. 131.

26. Quoted in Middlekauff, *Glorious Cause*, p. 182.

27. Quoted in Langguth, *Patriots*, p.105.

28. Quoted in Langguth, *Patriots*, p. 137.

29. Quoted in Langguth, *Patriots*, p. 137.

30. Jack P. Greene, ed., *Colonies to Nation, 1763–1789: A Documentary History of the American Revolution.* New York: W.W. Norton, 1975, p. 196.

Chapter Three: A Rebellion in Massachusetts, 1773–1775

31. Quoted in Harvey, *A Few Bloody Noses*, p. 112.

32. Quoted in Langguth, *Patriots*, p. 176.

33. Quoted in Langguth, *Patriots*, p. 177.

34. Quoted in Langguth, *Patriots*, p. 181.

35. Quoted in Langguth, *Patriots*, p. 181.

36. Quoted in Commager, *Documents of American History*, p. 71.

37. Quoted in Bobrick, *Angel in the Whirlwind*, p. 92.

38. Quoted in Bobrick, *Angel in the Whirlwind*, p. 95.

39. Quoted in Bobrick, *Angel in the Whirlwind*, p. 93.

40. Quoted in Greene, *Colonies to Nation*, p. 249.

41. Quoted in Middlekauff, *Glorious Cause*, p. 262.

42. Quoted in Harvey, *A Few Bloody Noses*, p. 99.

43. George F. Scheer and Hugh F. Rankin, eds., *Rebels and Redcoats: The American Revolution Through the Eyes of Those Who Fought and Lived It.* New York: De Capo, 1957, p. 20.

44. Quoted in Scheer and Rankin, *Rebels and Redcoats*, p. 21.

45. Quoted in Langguth, *Patriots*, p. 240.

46. Quoted in Scheer and Rankin, *Rebels and Redcoats*, p. 34.

47. Esmond Wright, ed., *The Fire of Liberty: The American War of Independence Seen Through the Eyes of the Men and Women, the Statesmen and Soldiers Who Fought It.* New York: St. Martin's, 1983, p. 25.

48. Quoted in Wright, *Fire of Liberty*, p. 26.

49. Quoted in Wright, *Fire of Liberty*, p. 28.

Chapter Four: Victory, Defeat, and a Declaration, 1775–1776

50. Steven Rosswurm, *Arms, Country, and Class: The Philadelphia Militia and the "Lower Sort" During the American Revolution.* New Brunswick, NJ: Rutgers University Press, 1987, p. 49

51. Quoted in Middlekauff, *Glorious Cause*, p. 28.

52. Quoted in Scheer and Rankin, *Rebels and Redcoats*, p. 62.

53. Quoted in Scheer and Rankin, *Rebels and Redcoats*, p. 62.

54. Quoted in Scheer and Rankin, *Rebels and Redcoats*, p. 128.

55. Quoted in Greene, *Colonies to Nation*, p. 259.
56. Harvey, *A Few Bloody Noses*, p. 199.
57. Quoted in Greene, *Colonies to Nation*, p. 270.
58. Quoted in Greene, *Colonies to Nation*, p. 277.
59. Quoted in Greene, *Colonies to Nation*, p. 278.
60. Quoted in Greene, *Colonies to Nation*, p. 284.
61. Quoted in Greene, *Colonies to Nation*, p. 297.
62. Quoted in Scheer and Rankin, *Rebels and Redcoats*, p. 166.
63. Quoted in Wright, *Fire of Liberty*, p. 72.
64. Quoted in Greene, *Colonies to Nation*, p. 406.
65. Quoted in Langguth, *Patriots*, p. 393.

Chapter Five: South from Saratoga, 1777–1779

66. Quoted in Middlekauff, *Glorious Cause*, p. 372.
67. Quoted in Middlekauff, *Glorious Cause*, p. 385.
68. Quoted in Wright, *Fire of Liberty*, p. 94.
69. Quoted in Scheer and Rankin, *Rebels and Redcoats*, p. 275.
70. Quoted in Scheer and Rankin, *Rebels and Redcoats*, p. 276.
71. Quoted in Langguth, *Patriots*, p. 456.
72. Quoted in Langguth, *Patriots*, p. 451.
73. Quoted in Commager, *Documents of American History*, p. 106.
74. Quoted in Commager, *Documents of American History*, p. 107.
75. Quoted in Scheer and Rankin, *Rebels and Redcoats*, p. 390.
76. Quoted in Middlekauff, *Glorious Cause*, p. 437.
77. Quoted in Bobrick, *Angel in the Whirlwind*, p. 373.
78. Quoted in Bobrick, *Angel in the Whirlwind*, p. 373.
79. Quoted in Harvey, *A Few Bloody Noses*, p. 329.

Chapter Six: The Road to Yorktown, 1780–1781

80. Quoted in Wright, *Fire of Liberty*, p. 183.
81. Quoted in Harvey, *A Few Bloody Noses*, pp. 331–32.
82. Quoted in Harvey, *A Few Bloody Noses*, p. 333.
83. Quoted in Scheer and Rankin, *Rebels and Redcoats*, p. 410.
84. Quoted in Langguth, *Patriots*, p. 504.
85. Quoted in Langguth, *Patriots*, p. 509.
86. Quoted in Harvey, *A Few Bloody Noses*, p. 369.
87. Bobrick, *Angel in the Whirlwind*, p. 433.
88. Quoted in Wright, *Fire of Liberty*, p. 232.
89. Quoted in Wright, *Fire of Liberty*, p. 233.
90. Quoted in Harvey, *A Few Bloody Noses*, p. 405.
91. Quoted in Langguth, *Patriots*, p. 540.

Epilogue: Novus Ordo Seclorum: A New Order of the Ages, 1781–1789

92. John Shy, *A People Numerous and Armed: Reflections on the Military*

Struggle for American Independence. Ann Arbor: University of Michigan Press, 1990, p. 205.

93. Geoffrey Perret, *A Country Made by War: From the Revolution to Vietnam—The Story of America's Rise to Power.* New York: Random House, 1989, p. 69.

94. Quoted in Greene, *Colonies to Nation,* p. 507.

95. Quoted in Greene, *Colonies to Nation,* p. 508.

For Further Reading

Books

Marc Aronson, *The Real Revolution: The Global Story of American Independence*. New York: Clarion, 2005. *The Real Revolution* sets the event in its proper global context by examining it as a world war involving participants other than the Americans and Great Britain.

Benson Bobrick, *Fight for Freedom: The American Revolutionary War*. New York: Atheneum, 2004. Bobrick's book is a well-illustrated narrative of the Revolution with a useful "Quick Facts" section.

Cynthia A. Kierner, *Revolutionary America, 1750–1815: Sources and Interpretations*. New Jersey: Prentice Hall, 2002. This is a valuable collection of primary source documents and accompanying essays.

Jim Murphy, *A Young Patriot: The American Revolution As Experienced by One Boy*. New York: Clarion, 1998. Murphy tells the true story of a fifteen-year-old boy who fights in the Continental army.

Ann Rinaldi, *Cast Two Shadows: The American Revolution in the South*. San Diego: Harcourt, 1998. A work of historical fiction, *Cast Two Shadows* is about a young southern girl's struggle to keep her family together as it splits between loyalism and rebellion.

Documentaries/Films

The American Revolution. History Channel, 2000. Reenactments and celebrity voice-overs are included in this documentary along with a solid narration of events.

Benedict Arnold: A Question of Honor. A&E Home Video, 2003. The infamous traitor's story is the subject of this film. It is an evenhanded presentation of Arnold's career and the events surrounding his attempt to betray West Point to the British.

The Crossing. A&E Home Video, 2003. *The Crossing* recreates George Washington's crossing of the Delaware River and defeat of the Hessians in December 1776.

Liberty! The American Revolution. Middlemarch Films, 1997. This is a documentary that provides a good chronological history of the Revolution.

Web Sites

The American Revolution (www.americanrevolution.com). For general information and an introduction to the major developments, this site is valuable.

The American Revolution Home Page
(www.americanrevwar.homestead.com/
files/INDEX2.HTM). The American Revolution Home Page is an electronic encyclopedia, covering events and personalities, with a Quick Reference section.

The History Place (www.historyplace.
com/unitedstates/revolution). This
site offers a very good timeline of key
events in the American Revolution. It
is easy to use and very informative.

Index

Picture Credits

Cover: Lithograph of The Spirit of 1776, c. 1880 by A.M. Willard, photograph, © CORBIS

© Bettmann/CORBIS, 8(lower), 9(lower), 20, 43, 44, 50, 55, 57, 61, 80

© CORBIS, 11, 28, 68, 77, 81, 84, 85, 89

© Kevin Fleming/CORBIS, 47

© Dave G. Howser/CORBIS, 52

© Francis G. Mayer/CORBIS, 58

© Leonard de Silva/CORBIS, 54

© Stapleton Collection/CORBIS, 28

Getty Images, 9(upper), 75

MPI/Getty Images, 23, 53, 59, 70

The Library of Congress, 8(upper), 16, 21, 41, 51, 64, 76

The National Archives, 19, 33, 35, 38, 66

About the Author

John Davenport holds a PhD in history from the University of Connecticut and currently teaches at Corte Madera School in Portola Valley, California. Davenport is the author of several biographies and books on American historical geography for young readers. He lives in San Carlos, California, with his wife Jennifer and his sons William and Andrew.